# Let the Word Become Life in Your Life

## A Step-by-Step Guide to Have, Be, and Do Everything the Bible Promises

It's time to break free from the disappointment caused by years of unfulfilled expectations in your Faith. Please don't allow it to hinder your progress any longer.

### Bishop Bill Anderson Th.D.

## VIDEO SUMMARY

Imagine having a personal conversation with the author, who guides you through the book's most crucial points and shares his intentions behind writing it.

This video summary bridges the gap between author and reader, creating a unique connection that enhances your reading experience.

This video provides valuable tips on effectively saving time and acquiring knowledge and insights while reading this book.

## BishopBillAnderson.org/video

# DOWNLOAD THE AUDIOBOOK FREE

To show my gratitude for your purchase, I am offering you the Audiobook version completely FREE!

The audio version is an absolute must-have for those who spend considerable time in their vehicles or enjoy walking while listening.

## BishopBillAnderson.org/audio

Copyright Bishop Bill Anderson © 2023

All rights reserved. No part of this book may be reproduced, stored in a retrieval system, or transmitted in any form or by any means, electronic, mechanical, photocopying, recording, public performances, or otherwise, without written permission of Bishop Bill Anderson except for brief quotations embodied in critical articles or reviews. All scripture references are taken from the King James Version of the Bible unless otherwise noted.

The Authorized (King James) Version of the Bible (the KJV), the rights in which are vested in the Crown in the United Kingdom, is reproduced here by permission of the Crown's patentee, Cambridge University Press. The Cambridge KJV text, including paragraphing, is reproduced here by permission of Cambridge University Press.

Scripture taken from THE AMPLIFIED BIBLE, Old Testament copyright ©1965, 1987 by the Zondervan Corporation. The Amplified New Testament copyright ©1958, 1987 by the Lockman Foundation. Used by permission.

Scripture in italics, bold, or underlined is for the author's emphasis.

ISBN: 979-8-89109-361-4 - paperback
ISBN: 979-8-89109-362-1 - ebook
ISBN: 979-8-89109-432-1 - hardcover

Author Name
Bishop Bill Anderson Th.D.

Book Title
Let The Word Become Life in Your Life

Book Subtitle
A Step-by-Step Guide to Have, Be, and Do Everything the Bible Says Starting Today!

# ACKNOWLEDGMENT

First, I want to thank my precious Heavenly Father, who has been faithful to love, correct, instruct, and discipline me with patience throughout my faith journey. I am forever grateful He has entrusted me with the message, *Let the Word Become Life in Your Life* which is all about people experiencing the blessings of applying His Word in their life. While many view God as a mean judge, He is a loving Heavenly Father who wants His children to be blessed, healthy, prosperous, and discover their purpose in life.

I want to thank Rev. Connie Anderson, my amazing wife, friend, partner, and helpmate in every aspect of life and our international ministry. I am forever grateful for her unwavering support, dedication, and countless hours spent finishing projects and spreading the message of vision, hope, and love to those in need.

I also want to thank those in the family of God who serve alongside me. To my ministers, staff, and congregation of BAM International, I could never express enough thanks for all your hard work since planting the church in 1981.

I want to thank my son, Pastor Aaron Anderson, for diligently recording my sermons over the years and for continuing to spread the message of "Letting the Word become life in your life." Seeing him answering the call to pastor and minister to the next generation brings me great joy.

I want to thank my twelve-year-old grandson, Liam Anderson, for his passion and fantastic ability to play drums during our church services. He has already begun to preach the same message to his generation. His devotion has not only captured the hearts of our congregation but has also inspired and touched the lives of his fellow youth.

# ABOUT THE AUTHOR

Bill Anderson was born on March 21, 1954, and felt a calling from God in 1976. He graduated with honors from Carmel Bible Institute in 1978 and was the Honor Student from Supernatural Ministries Training Institute in 1984. Bill is an affiliate member and former District director for Michigan with the International Convention of Faith Ministries, Inc. He was also invited to join Bishops worldwide to promote dialogue and unity between historic and renewed churches. In 2001, Bill was ordained a Bishop with ICCC (International Communion of Charismatic Churches) to help develop schools, model ministries, and media outlets.

Bishop Anderson has established Bill Anderson Ministries, Inc., an outreach ministry sending numerous evangelistic teams to other churches, the streets, and the mission fields. He is the Founder and Pastor of BAM International, a thriving, growing church in Sandusky, Michigan. BAM TV, the internet church, has reached several countries and over forty states in the USA weekly. He is the President of the Sandusky Area Association of Churches; together, they promote unity to further the cause of Christ's Kingdom by providing combined community services, financial help, outreach, and evangelism.

World missions are in the heart of this man of God. He does his part to "go into all the world and make disciples." Bishop Bill has already ministered extensively throughout Central and South America, Canada, Europe, Cuba, Ukraine, Germany, Portugal, Australia, and Africa. He has ministered before the masses and before those in the jungle huts.

Bishop Anderson is an Ordained Minister of the Gospel. He walks in the office of an apostle with the gift of teaching. In addition to writing the four-year curriculum for BAM University, he has authored several books.

His wife, Rev. Connie, is the Administrator of BAM University Training Centers worldwide and the Director of BAM Publications. As an apostle and prophet team, they travel worldwide, establishing the believer and encouraging the Local Churches.

Bishop Bill Anderson is a man of God who knows the signs of the time and has the Word for the hour. His heart is to bring the Word of God alive so that those who hear it can apply it to their lives and live it. You will be refreshed as you hear his message to the Body of Christ. This message enables people everywhere to "Let the Word Become Life in Your Life.

# DEDICATION

It is with great honor and gratitude that I humbly dedicate this book to the fathers in my faith who have been a shining example of true dedication to the Lord and His ministry. Their unwavering commitment and tireless efforts in spreading love, compassion, and hope have left an indelible mark on my heart and soul. I am forever grateful for their guidance, wisdom, and unwavering support. May their dedication serve as a constant reminder of the boundless possibilities that can be achieved through the power of faith and devotion to a higher calling.

I want to dedicate this to those hungry for the Word of God and the desire to "let the Word become life in your life" and those interested and ready for an encounter with the only true living God. Your desire to have, be, and do everything the Bible says keeps me going.

# FOREWORD
## Dr. Mark T. Barclay

My entire life was changed when I first heard a message preached that taught me to trust God and His Word—a message that exalted the Word of God (the Holy Scriptures), a message that said, "If God said it in the Bible, you can take it to the bank!" That message was the word of faith, and as it unfolded and developed, it brought much light to me and I began to remodel my entire life.

This message of faith gave me many insights about different aspects of life. It taught me about my mouth and how I should and shouldn't use it. It taught me about my heart and how it could be filled with faith, or filled with doubt and unbelief. It taught me about my head and my mind, and whether I was renewing it or not. It caused to me examine whether I was thinking like the Bible (the Word of God), or still thinking and reasoning like a mere human… and on and on.

Bill Anderson has done a tremendous job to lay out the truths in this book, a topic at a time, so the reader can easily understand them. In fact, every area I mentioned above is covered and explained, and more. This is the way to live on Planet Earth. This book will teach you to trust God, to be more than a conqueror, to understand how God meant for us to live on this planet, and how to defeat the enemies of our lives.

Bill has always had a unique way to present the message with enough simplicity that all can understand yet enough meat for even the mature. I believe you will find yourself using this book as a reference guide for your future as you go back and refer to it time and again to be refreshed about these most crucial doctrines and precious insights.

Job well done, Bill! May every Christian everywhere get a copy.

Mark T. Barclay

PREACHER OF RIGHTEOUSNESS

# TABLE OF CONTENTS

**ACKNOWLEDGMENT** . . . . . . . . . . . . . . . . . . . . . . . . .v

**ABOUT THE AUTHOR**. . . . . . . . . . . . . . . . . . . . . . . .vii

**DEDICATION** . . . . . . . . . . . . . . . . . . . . . . . . . . . . ix

**FOREWORD by** Dr. Mark T. Barclay. . . . . . . . . . . . . . . . . . xi

**Introduction Sermon in a Phrase —
Let The Word Become Life in Your Life** . . . . . . . . . . . . . . . .1

**CHAPTER 1: Three Aspects of Faith** . . . . . . . . . . . . . . . . .5
    What Is Faith?. . . . . . . . . . . . . . . . . . . . . . . . . . . 5
    Testing Your Faith . . . . . . . . . . . . . . . . . . . . . . . . 8
    Three Aspects of Faith . . . . . . . . . . . . . . . . . . . . . .10
    Questions: . . . . . . . . . . . . . . . . . . . . . . . . . . . .16
    Prayer Focus: . . . . . . . . . . . . . . . . . . . . . . . . . .16

**CHAPTER 2: The Law of Faith** . . . . . . . . . . . . . . . . . . .19
    The Application of the Law . . . . . . . . . . . . . . . . . . .20
    Saved through Faith . . . . . . . . . . . . . . . . . . . . . . .21
    Through Faith, We Establish the Law . . . . . . . . . . . . . . .23
    Questions: . . . . . . . . . . . . . . . . . . . . . . . . . . . .30
    Prayer Focus: . . . . . . . . . . . . . . . . . . . . . . . . . .31

**CHAPTER 3: The Just Shall Live by Faith** . . . . . . . . . . . . . .33
    What It Means to Live by Faith . . . . . . . . . . . . . . . . .34
    Living by Faith. . . . . . . . . . . . . . . . . . . . . . . . . .37
    Faith Can Be Seen . . . . . . . . . . . . . . . . . . . . . . . .41
    Questions: . . . . . . . . . . . . . . . . . . . . . . . . . . . .45
    Prayer Focus: . . . . . . . . . . . . . . . . . . . . . . . . . .45

**CHAPTER 4: Five Levels of Faith** . . . . . . . . . . . . . . . . . .47
    Level One — The Measure of Faith. . . . . . . . . . . . . . . .47
    Level Two — No Faith . . . . . . . . . . . . . . . . . . . . .49

Level Three — Little Faith . . . . . . . . . . . . . . . . . . . . . .50
Level Four — Great Faith . . . . . . . . . . . . . . . . . . . . . . .53
Where Are You At? . . . . . . . . . . . . . . . . . . . . . . . . . . .55
Level Five — Full of Faith . . . . . . . . . . . . . . . . . . . . . .57
Progress Isn't a Straight Line . . . . . . . . . . . . . . . . . . . .58
Questions: . . . . . . . . . . . . . . . . . . . . . . . . . . . . . . . .59
Prayer Focus: . . . . . . . . . . . . . . . . . . . . . . . . . . . . . .59

## CHAPTER 5: The Process of Faith . . . . . . . . . . . . . . . . . . . . 61
The Six Steps in the Process of Faith . . . . . . . . . . . . . . . .62
A Word of Wisdom to Keep Your Momentum . . . . . . . . . . .70
Questions: . . . . . . . . . . . . . . . . . . . . . . . . . . . . . . . .70
Prayer Focus: . . . . . . . . . . . . . . . . . . . . . . . . . . . . . .71

## CHAPTER 6: 36 Blessings of Faith . . . . . . . . . . . . . . . . . . . 73
Salvation . . . . . . . . . . . . . . . . . . . . . . . . . . . . . . . . .74
Healing . . . . . . . . . . . . . . . . . . . . . . . . . . . . . . . . . .76
Whole . . . . . . . . . . . . . . . . . . . . . . . . . . . . . . . . . . .77
Righteousness . . . . . . . . . . . . . . . . . . . . . . . . . . . . . .77
Speak to Mountains . . . . . . . . . . . . . . . . . . . . . . . . . .78
Purified Hearts . . . . . . . . . . . . . . . . . . . . . . . . . . . . .79
Churches Established . . . . . . . . . . . . . . . . . . . . . . . . .79
Sanctification . . . . . . . . . . . . . . . . . . . . . . . . . . . . . .80
Testimony . . . . . . . . . . . . . . . . . . . . . . . . . . . . . . . .80
Won't Fail . . . . . . . . . . . . . . . . . . . . . . . . . . . . . . . .81
Strong . . . . . . . . . . . . . . . . . . . . . . . . . . . . . . . . . . .81
Miracles . . . . . . . . . . . . . . . . . . . . . . . . . . . . . . . . .82
Children of Abraham . . . . . . . . . . . . . . . . . . . . . . . . .82
Justified . . . . . . . . . . . . . . . . . . . . . . . . . . . . . . . . .83
Strong and Not Stagger . . . . . . . . . . . . . . . . . . . . . . . .84
Access . . . . . . . . . . . . . . . . . . . . . . . . . . . . . . . . . . .84
Wiser than the Wisdom of Men . . . . . . . . . . . . . . . . . .85
Walk by Faith . . . . . . . . . . . . . . . . . . . . . . . . . . . . . .85
Indwelling . . . . . . . . . . . . . . . . . . . . . . . . . . . . . . . .85
Shield of Faith . . . . . . . . . . . . . . . . . . . . . . . . . . . . .86
Nourished and Fed . . . . . . . . . . . . . . . . . . . . . . . . . .86
Creative Words . . . . . . . . . . . . . . . . . . . . . . . . . . . . .86
Inherit Promises . . . . . . . . . . . . . . . . . . . . . . . . . . . .87

Substance and Evidence . . . . . . . . . . . . . . . . . . . . . . . . . . . . . . . .87
Please God . . . . . . . . . . . . . . . . . . . . . . . . . . . . . . . . . . . . . . . . . .88
Patience . . . . . . . . . . . . . . . . . . . . . . . . . . . . . . . . . . . . . . . . . . . .88
Salvation of Your Soul . . . . . . . . . . . . . . . . . . . . . . . . . . . . . . . . . .89
Victory That Overcomes the World . . . . . . . . . . . . . . . . . . . . . . . .89
Powerful Prayer Life . . . . . . . . . . . . . . . . . . . . . . . . . . . . . . . . . . .90
Unity . . . . . . . . . . . . . . . . . . . . . . . . . . . . . . . . . . . . . . . . . . . . . . .90
Questions: . . . . . . . . . . . . . . . . . . . . . . . . . . . . . . . . . . . . . . . . . .91
Prayer Focus: . . . . . . . . . . . . . . . . . . . . . . . . . . . . . . . . . . . . . . . .92

## CHAPTER 7: Keep the Faith . . . . . . . . . . . . . . . . . . . . . . . . 93
Questions: . . . . . . . . . . . . . . . . . . . . . . . . . . . . . . . . . . . . . . . . . 103
Prayer Focus: . . . . . . . . . . . . . . . . . . . . . . . . . . . . . . . . . . . . . . 104

## CHAPTER 8: The Holy Spirit Works in The Five Levels of Faith . . . 105
The Five Levels of Faith and the Work of the Holy Spirit . . . . . . . . . . 105
Questions: . . . . . . . . . . . . . . . . . . . . . . . . . . . . . . . . . . . . . . . . . 117
Prayer Focus: . . . . . . . . . . . . . . . . . . . . . . . . . . . . . . . . . . . . . . 118

## CHAPTER 9: Demons and The Three Aspects of Faith . . . . . . . . 119
Principalities, Powers, Rulers, Wicked Spirits . . . . . . . . . . . . . . 119
Three Temptations of Jesus . . . . . . . . . . . . . . . . . . . . . . . . . . . 124
Temptations Come in Three Areas . . . . . . . . . . . . . . . . . . . . . . 126
Questions: . . . . . . . . . . . . . . . . . . . . . . . . . . . . . . . . . . . . . . . . . 132
Prayer Focus: . . . . . . . . . . . . . . . . . . . . . . . . . . . . . . . . . . . . . . 133

## CHAPTER 10: Faith Scatters the Enemies . . . . . . . . . . . . . . . 135
Let God Arise . . . . . . . . . . . . . . . . . . . . . . . . . . . . . . . . . . . . . 135
Faith Can Scatter the Six Enemies of God . . . . . . . . . . . . . . . . 139
As You Go . . . . . . . . . . . . . . . . . . . . . . . . . . . . . . . . . . . . . . . . 143
Questions: . . . . . . . . . . . . . . . . . . . . . . . . . . . . . . . . . . . . . . . . . 145
Prayer Focus: . . . . . . . . . . . . . . . . . . . . . . . . . . . . . . . . . . . . . . 145

## CHAPTER 11: The Communication of Your Faith . . . . . . . . . . . 147
Corrupt Communication . . . . . . . . . . . . . . . . . . . . . . . . . . . . . 149
Simplifying Your Communication . . . . . . . . . . . . . . . . . . . . . . 153
Correct Bible Interpretation . . . . . . . . . . . . . . . . . . . . . . . . . . . 156
Communication Is Two-Way . . . . . . . . . . . . . . . . . . . . . . . . . . 158
Listen Before You Communicate . . . . . . . . . . . . . . . . . . . . . . 160
Communication the Lord's Way . . . . . . . . . . . . . . . . . . . . . . . 161

    God's Word in Our Mouth............................. 162
    Questions:............................................ 163
    Prayer Focus:......................................... 164

**CHAPTER 12: Faith and the Lord of the Harvest............ 167**
    Seed Time Harvest..................................... 167
    Messages from the Harvest............................. 169
    Whatever We Sow....................................... 179
    Understanding the Kingdom of God...................... 182
    When to Use Parables.................................. 187
    Parables Teaching That Temptation Will Come but Not from God....... 188
    By Faith, Begin to Praise God for Our Harvest......... 191
    Questions:............................................ 191
    Prayer Focus:......................................... 192

**CHAPTER 13: Life After Death............................ 193**
    What Is Life?......................................... 193
    What Is Death?........................................ 195
    Is There Life Before and After Death?................. 197
    Eternal Life and the God Kind of Life................. 200
    The Power of Death.................................... 203
    We Will Overcome Death................................ 207
    How Can You Know If You Have Life After Death?........ 208
    Questions:............................................ 209
    Prayer Focus:......................................... 209

**CHAPTER 14: Faith for Forgiveness....................... 211**
    The Power of Forgiveness.............................. 212
    Where Do We Start with Forgiveness?................... 221
    Questions:............................................ 223
    Prayer Focus:......................................... 224

**CHAPTER 15: Faith for the Future........................ 225**
    Carve Out Rivers...................................... 226
    What Is the Church Doing Today?....................... 231
    How Far Downstream Can You See?....................... 231
    Faith for the Future Redemption, Creation, and Reset.. 235
    Questions:............................................ 239
    Prayer Focus:......................................... 239

# Introduction
# Sermon in a Phrase — Let The Word Become Life in Your Life

I'm so pleased to be able to share this message with you today. I'm approaching about 12,000 sermons I've preached in my forty years of ministry. I've always started my sermon the same way for all those years. First, I ask, "How many have a Bible?" I then ask people to say this with me: "I can have everything this Bible says I can have, I can be everything this Bible says I can be, and I can do everything this Bible says I can do. Today, I will let this Word become life in my life!" This confession has been the foundation phrase for every message I've preached. I'm here today to clarify why this is a must foundational phrase for developing a lifestyle of living by faith in every area of your life.

Let me give you a little history of how this phrase came to be. I grew up in the church and acquired all the sticky stars beside my name because I memorized the scriptures. They crowned me king of Bible camp because I memorized more scriptures than anyone else. However, I became disillusioned at church because I saw that the lives of some of the leadership and congregants weren't different from anybody else's. I thought this faith thing wasn't working! All these scriptures were not working in their lives. Have you ever felt like this Christianity thing is not working, the church is boring, the sermons are irrelevant to your life, and so what is the use?

I felt like there must be more, so I thought I would move on in my life. I took a seven-year lap and tried everything the world had to offer. I became a professional sinner and was good at it. I became successful and accumulated a lot of "stuff" and popularity, but I felt empty and realized something was missing. I decided to try God again. So one day, I was at the beach reading a book about the Bible, trying to make sense of this Christianity thing. I put my hand in the sand and realized I could not count the grains of sand in my hand. Then, I could not count the grains of sand that fell out of my hand, then I looked at the beach and could not count the grains of sand on the beach. Wow. It was then that it happened. I heard the voice of God speak to me audibly. He said, "Bill, I know how many hairs are on your head!" I knew it was God because I had memorized the scripture: *But even the very hairs of your head are all numbered. Fear not . . .* (Luke 12:7). Everything changed at that moment! I knew God was real; He knew me and wanted a relationship with me.

On that day, the Word I had memorized got out of my head and went into my heart. Everything changed that day. Are you with me? Everything changed that day — my whole life, my reason for living, my purpose in life — and that began forty years ago; my walk of faith hasn't faltered and is still there today.

The next day, I was back at my job as a dairy farmer. I had a bulk tank and a pipeline milker, so the milk piped to the milk house, and it would drain into a bulk tank, but I always would turn the pipe a little sideways and dip it down because I could get a few more drops. Being the reasonable, conservative, and analytical person I was, I figured that a few more drops every milking would add up with the price of milk. While doing that, I realized the milk was coming from one place to another. God spoke to me again, and He said this: "Let the Word become life in your life." I realized that just like the milk was moving from one place to another, the word of God had to move from my head to my heart and life. I heard it audibly, thus the tagline or the phrase for my ministry that I didn't even know I had yet.

For the last forty years, I've preached "Let the Word Become Life in Your Life" from that moment on. The message hasn't changed even though the subject matter may be different. The concept is that if you can find a promise in the Bible, if it is in the Word, then you can have it, you can be it, you can do it, so let it become life in your life. Am I making any sense to you now?

When I would run into people I had seen before, even years later, they'd come up to me and say, "I'm letting the Word become life in my life." When someone mentioned my name, "Let the Word become life in your life" was also mentioned, and I became synonymous with this phrase.

I want to tell you that this was a phrase God gave me; I hadn't decided to sit down and brainstorm a good slogan and a good tagline for my ministry. As I said, I had this phrase before I even knew I had a ministry. The Word became life in my life. He was telling me what happened to me that day. I just wanted you to know where it came from: it came from God. This is why the phrase sticks in people's minds — because it was a Word from God, not a man's tagline.

This was the frustration I had felt with the church in my earlier years: the Word didn't seem to affect people's lives. I understand the frustration of many people who know what the Bible says, but it's not life in their life. That was why I had left. I knew what the Bible said, but it wasn't "life in my life." It wasn't working for me, and it wasn't real to me. But, when it became real, my whole life changed. Because I have and am still letting His Word become "life in my life," my faith has stayed strong for forty years. I'm healthy, I'm still blessed, I'm still prosperous, things are well, I have no pain in my body whatsoever, and I feel healthy even in my early seventies.

I pray that the Word will become "life in your life" when you hear this message! As you let the Word become life in your life throughout the topics in this book, my prayer is that you will enjoy the promises of God, stay strong, and that your faith will never fail. So are you ready to start this fantastic journey?

**In His Service,**

**Bishop Bill Anderson**

# CHAPTER 1

# Three Aspects of Faith

The first thing we need to understand is faith. Many people have a weird idea of what faith is. Let's find out what the Bible says: *so then Faith cometh* [you're not born with Faith, Faith has to come] *by hearing* (Romans 10:17). The verse continues and says, *and hearing by the word of God.* There are two hearings in this verse, and I want to separate those for a moment.

## What Is Faith?

### Faith Comes by Hearing

Let's just look at that part of the phrase and discuss the faith that comes because you hear something and believe it. This type of faith is a natural process that happens 24/7 in your life. For example, when the TV advertises something, you listen to it, think you need it, get your credit card out and charge it, and soon you will have it. Whatever you hear becomes life in your life. Or take the messages you heard as a child. Did you hear that you're stupid? That you'll never amount to anything? Or did you hear the flip side? That you're a perfect angel and never have to change. That can be just as bad for other reasons. Maybe you grew up in a positive atmosphere and heard words of affirmation that caused you to press into being the best you can be. Regardless, pretty soon, you believed what you heard. What you believe comes every day; faith is a natural process. I want you to understand that faith is not difficult to operate in because you already do it 24/7 in every area of your life.

When faith comes, it can be good or bad, but what you do with it is what you believe.

## Hearing by the Word of God

The other part of the phrase is not just about hearing natural everyday things, but the second hearing, the Greek word — *akauo* brings out the idea of understanding. It opens our minds up a little bit to realize there is a natural hearing and a spiritual hearing. Faith comes in the same way with God as it does in the natural world — by hearing. You've probably heard your parents say, "Oh, be careful little ears, what you hear! Be careful what you hear from your peers, in the church, from Christians, and from the pulpit; it may not be the true Word of God." Another phrase you have probably heard is, "Believe nothing you hear and half of what you see." Someone might say the sun is not shining today; well, you might have to get up in an airplane and get above the obstructions of the clouds, but it's shining today. Faith understands the Word of God. If I know and understand the Word of God, then no one can tell me the sun's not shining today because I know it is. It's just cloudy, and yes, there's something in the way.

Let's take what I was told forty years ago. I heard God say, by His stripes, you were healed (1 Peter 2:24). That day, I just believed that, and I was healed. Then other times over the years, I have had some cloudy days, some symptoms, some obstructions, and some thoughts, but I would get in my little spiritual airplane and get above all that doubt. And guess what I found out? I was still healed. I didn't have to get healed; I *was* healed. You might have to get past some obstructions to see, but that's called understanding the Word.

Once you understand the Word, it's tough for the devil to lie to you anymore. I read this scripture that *the devil comes not but for to steal, kill and destroy* (John 10:10). I understood that if the devil himself is coming to steal something in my life, I must already have it. What a revelation to me! So, every time the devil comes with sickness or symptoms or anything else, I know he's trying to steal something I already have, which is healing. I have health; he's just trying to steal it. That means I don't have to believe "for" healing; why would I believe "for" healing if I already have it? Wow!

Do you see, faith gets a little weird? The devil tries to twist it around. An example is when he said to Eve *if you eat out of that tree, you will be like God* (Genesis 3:5). Wait for a minute. God already made Adam and Eve in his image and in his likeness and placed them there to give them dominion over the earth. They already were like God. Adam and Eve lost their likeness to God as soon as their mindset shifted. When their perspective changed, they believed they did not share God's traits. The Devil just stole that understanding from them with a mindset change. We need to find out what we have, and once we find out what we have, the devil will not take it from us because we know it's ours and he's just a thief. *The thief cometh not, but for to steal, and to kill, and to destroy: I am come that they might have life, and that they might have it more abundantly* (John 10:10).

Faith comes by hearing what God has to say. As I said, I don't try to believe "for" healing because I know and believe what God has said about healing. I don't believe "for" money because I believe what God has said about money. Please understand that this faith walk is much simpler than what we make it. It's just simply this: God said it, I believe it, and that settles it because His Word is a higher authority than any other words. The sun is shining, but it's cloudy, and we must overcome the obstacles of doubt, disbelief, and the lack of understanding of God's words.

## Testing Your Faith

When the test of doubt comes, you will immediately discover what you do or do not believe. Tests are not destructive; instead, they simply show you what you don't know yet. With His stripes, I'm healed. When the symptoms come, we'll see if you believe that.

Even His disciples had moments where they didn't always believe. Yet, the disciples were men of faith; correct? Jesus picked twelve disciples who were purported to be men of faith. He said, "Let's get in the boat; we're going to the other side." They agreed. "Yes, sir, we're going to the other side in Jesus's name."

Jesus was comfortable going to the other side because God told him to. He rested on what God said and slept in the boat. A little obstacle came up like waves coming over the ship's edge, and the giant faith disciples went to Jesus and said, "We're all going to die; help me, Jesus." Now that's funny. The faith giants had significant doubts, but that's what we do when we get sick. We go to Jesus and ask Him for help. When we have a problem, that's the first thing out of our mouths. "Help me, Jesus." Jesus got up and rebuked the storm, which was simply an obstacle to the command of God to go to the other side. Look what Jesus said to His disciples, "Why do you still not have faith?"

Jesus seemed to think, "Well, God said we're going to the other side. Why didn't you speak to the obstacle? Why didn't you say something? Well, because they didn't believe that they had any authority to do so." Do we believe we have the authority to speak to the storms we encounter? We need to believe we have the authority to speak to any obstacle that is trying to prevent us from doing what God has told us to do.

Faith does not mean you have to be a super spiritual being. You simply need to trust what God has said and speak to any obstacles that may be in the way.

If faith comes by hearing the Word of God, how often do you hear the Word instead of other words? Friends, you hear other words all day long, but are you going to limit a fifteen-minute sermonette on Sunday to offset the bombardment of the other words? When I first was in the ministry, we used to have 120-minute cassettes. People would sit for 120 minutes hearing the Word. Yet, today if it's more than 15 minutes, they're out of there. Faith is not going to come if we don't hear it. If you've lost your hunger for the word of God, it's time to get hungry for your Bible again. *Blessed are they which do **hunger** and thirst after righteousness: for they shall be filled* (Matthew 5:6). Well then, if you are going to be filled with faith, you will have to get hungry again.

# Three Aspects of Faith

You need to apply the Three Aspects of Faith for the Word to become life in your life. If one of these is missing, you're not doing it, or you don't understand it, then your faith may fail.

The Three Aspects of Faith:

- **The Word of Faith** — *The Message*
- **The Law of Faith** — *The Application*
- **The Spirit of Faith** — *The Lifestyle*

<u>The Word of Faith—The Message</u>

The Word of Faith is the message. The message is not the sermon, illustration, or denomination. No, it is The Word of Faith with an emphasis on the Word. *What saith it?* ***The word is nigh thee, even in thy mouth, and in thy heart that is,*** ***the word of Faith*** *which we preach* (Romans 10:8). The Word must get past your ears and into your mouth and heart. It's not hard to get the everyday words in your mouth; you must listen to what somebody is saying and know what word is in their heart.

I'd rather you have three words of faith in your heart and mouth than forty in your head. I grew up with all of them in my head, but it did me no good until I got them in my mouth. You're changed forever as soon as one becomes life in your life. When The Word of Faith is in your heart, you believe it with everything in you, and no one can tell you anything different.

I will preach the Word, the whole Word, and nothing but the Word, so help me, God. I will preach the Word, not the

Reader's Digest, not the news, and not the chaos that's going on in the world. I've been to communist countries, and guess what? God is moving there in healing people and delivering people, so you don't have to vote God in for a move of God; you have to preach The Word of Faith, and people receive the blessings of God.

People have told me, "So, then, you're a word of faith church." I respond, "Well, we're not a word of doubt church." Over time, different people will see in the Word a revelation. Martin Luther one day noticed that in the Word, we are "saved by grace," which was revolutionary. Rev. Connie and I were in the church where Martin Luther nailed the 95 Theses on the door. He started a whole move of God with that one revelation, which eventually became the Lutheran churches. Charles Wesley came along and said, yes, we are "saved by grace," but there's holiness in the Bible, so then we got a whole holiness movement. William Brannon and others said that the Holy Ghost was available today, so we have Pentecostal churches. Kenneth Hagin saw faith in the Bible, and we have faith churches. Archbishop Earl Paulk said it's bigger than that; the Kingdom of God includes faith, healing, and dominion, so we have Kingdom churches. And on goes the story, but those revelations often become a camp unto themselves. So, what's BAM International, Bill Anderson Ministries Inc.? Well, we're Word of Faith, we're Pentecostal, we're saved by grace. We believe in holiness. We're kingdom. We are whatever the Word says we are, so what do we preach? We preach the Word about all those things.

## The Law of Faith—The Application

The Law of Faith is the application of the Word. In the phrase, "let the Word become life in *your* life," the word "let" means to obey. I need to let or obey The Word of Faith I have heard to become "life in my life."

Faith is a law; faith is a spiritually legal right that God has given us for certain things; it's a law that if you confess Jesus as your Lord, you will be saved and have eternal life, which is a legal thing.

This doesn't mean to boast when you're saved. *Where is boasting, then? It is excluded. By what law? Of works? Nay: but by the* **law of faith** (Romans 3:27).

How can we boast? You can't brag about being healed or boast that you're prosperous. It was simply the Word that did it; you were just smart enough to let it. *That your faith should not stand in the wisdom of men, but in the power of God* (1 Corinthians 2:5). The word power is "Dunamis" in Greek, and it means exceeding. His law is above every law. His Word is the final authority on anything. Anybody else can say whatever they want, but when God says it, that's the final authority; there is no higher law, as you can't take it to a higher court than God. Personally, I want to know what God says because that's the final authority. If God said it, I believe it, and that settles it.

God has established some laws, such as the law of gravity. Just step off the porch thinking you have one more step, and you'll discover that the law of gravity is still in process. The law of momentum is in operation when you're running, and you realize, *Oh my, that's a glass door, and it's not open.*

Examples of how The Law of Faith works:

- For God so loved the world, that he gave his only begotten Son, that ***whosoever believeth in him*** should not perish, ***but have everlasting life*** (John 3:16).

- Therefore, ***if any man be in Christ, he is a new creature: old things are passed away;*** behold, ***all things are become new*** (2 Corinthians 5:17).

- But he was wounded for our transgressions, he was bruised for our iniquities: the chastisement of our peace was upon him, and ***with his stripes, we are healed*** (Isaiah 53:5).

- Who his own self bare our sins in his own body on the tree, that we, being dead to sins, should live unto righteousness: ***and with his stripes we are healed*** (1 Peter 2:24).

- They shall take up serpents; and if they drink any deadly thing, it shall not hurt them; they shall ***lay hands on the sick, and they shall recover*** (Mark 16:18).

- For ***if ye forgive*** men their trespasses, ***your heavenly Father will also forgive you*** (Matthew 6:14).

- ***Give, and it shall be given unto you;*** good measure, pressed down, and shaken together, and running over, shall men give into your bosom. For with the same measure that ye mete withal, it shall be measured to you again (Luke 6:38).

- ***Bring ye all the tithes into the storehouse,*** that there may be meat in mine house, and prove me now herewith, saith the LORD of hosts, if ***I will not open you the windows of heaven***, and pour you out a blessing, that there shall not be room enough to receive it (Malachi 3:10).

As you can see, the Law of God backs each of these promises; when we operate in The Law of Faith and let or obey His Word, His law goes into effect, and He performs it.

Remember, the first Aspect of Faith is The Word of Faith, the message, and the second Aspect of Faith is The Law of Faith, the application. A powerful verse that combines them is But be ye doers of the word, and not hearers only, deceiving your own selves (James 1:22). If you do not operate in this Law of Faith, which is number two in the Three Aspects of Faith, that means you just heard The Word of Faith — making you a hearer only. Number two, you must do The Word of Faith; if you don't, you deceive yourself into believing you have it, yet there is no manifestation without the action. Be a hearer and a doer, and enjoy the blessing and promise of God.

## The Spirit of Faith — The Lifestyle

The Spirit of Faith, the lifestyle, is the last of the Three Aspects of Faith. This aspect is when you turn The Word of Faith and The Law of Faith into an everyday lifestyle. In the phrase, "let the Word become life in your life," the second life refers to what is now "live" in your life that has become an everyday living reality. The Apostle Paul writes to the Corinthians, *We having the same* **spirit of Faith**, *according as it is written, I believed, and therefore have I spoken; we also believe, and therefore speak* (2 Corinthians 4:13). We live this Bible. It's a lifestyle; it's not just a message. It's not just a legal thing. We live this.

The Spirit of Faith believes, speaks, and does what the Bible says. Again, Paul writes to the Galatians, *The just shall live by faith* (Galatians 3:11). The ones in right standing with God live by faith! We live by faith; we don't just visit it once in a while. We used to sing a song back in Sunday school class, "I Found a New Way of Living." Why did we forget it after the church meeting and return to the old way of living? Don't deceive yourself. This is not just a Sunday thing, but a lifestyle. The Apostle James gives us great wisdom: *Even so, Faith, if it hath not works, is dead, being alone* (James 2:17). We must do this until it has become a lifestyle. Finally, the Apostle Paul sums it all up in this verse: *If we live in the Spirit, let us also walk in the Spirit* (Galatians 5:25). We must get up every morning and decide that we're going to let the Word become life in our life.

I trust you have seen how each word in the phrase, "let the Word become life in your life" follows the Three Aspects of Faith:

- "The Word" is The Word of Faith
- "Let and become" is The Law of Faith
- "Your life" is The Spirit of Faith.

Move into The Spirit of Faith by being a cheerleader to yourself to get in the spirit. You can get into the Spirit by saying out loud: I can have, I can be, and I can do everything my Bible says, and today I'm going to let the Word become life in my life.

## Questions:

- What are the Three Aspects of Faith?
- How would you describe or explain The Word of Faith?
- Where can you hear The Word of Faith preached?
- How would you describe or explain The Law of Faith?
- How do many break The Law of Faith?
- How can our confession bring salvation to every area of our life? Healing, finances, favor, and problems in general.
- Have you ever considered that you were breaking The Law of Faith?
- How would you describe or explain The Spirit of Faith?
- How can we begin living in The Spirit of Faith?

## Prayer Focus:

- Pray that you will see and recognize the Three Aspects of Faith.
- Pray that you will once again hear, apply, and live the message of Faith.
- Pray that your ears will be open to hear The Word of Faith.
- Pray that you will be adamant about applying The Law of Faith with your every confession.
- Pray and thank the Lord that Faith is the higher law that supersedes all other laws.
- Pray and make your confessions according to the Word.

- Pray that you will make living by Faith a daily priority.
- Pray that the Holy Spirit will guard your lips and help you to keep your confessions aligned with the Word.
- Pray that all the ministers will continue to preach The Word of Faith.
- Pray that your life will be a testimony as you live and demonstrate The Word of Faith operating in your life.
- Pray that you will preach and speak The Word of Faith.

# CHAPTER 2

# The Law of Faith

As we begin this chapter, please read this confession aloud: *"I can have everything the Bible says I can have, I can be everything the Bible says I can be, and I can do everything the Bible says I can do. Today I'm going to let the Word become life in my life."*

I have found that many are struggling with their Faith because of one common missing aspect: The Law of Faith. We've already discussed this in the Three Aspects of Faith, but we need more in-depth teaching because the Law of Faith has been greatly misunderstood.

*Where is boasting, then? It is excluded. By what law? Of works? Nay: but by* **The Law of Faith** (Romans 3:27). The Apostle Paul clearly says that our Faith does not work by our works or fleshly effort. Our problem begins when we start trying to "work" our Faith and endeavor to make it happen in our self-effort. We strain, squint, sweat, and try to help God with our own ideas of Faith. Faith is a Law that God has established, is pleased when we walk in it, and He will back it in the legal courts of Heaven. Notice Paul says we won't be able to boast about it because it is not our self-effort; God is the one doing the work.

# The Application of the Law

Here are some definitions of law: A binding custom or practice of a community; a rule of conduct or action prescribed, formally recognized as binding or enforced by a controlling authority; the whole body of such customs, practices, or regulations. The courts exist to uphold, interpret, and apply the law.

Here are some application definitions: A formal request to an authority for something, the action of putting something into operation, the act of putting it to a particular use or purpose, and the act of requesting and entering into a legal transaction.

With the above definitions, we can say that as a Christian community, we have rules of conduct formally recognized as binding and enforced by our controlling authority, Almighty God, in the Courts of Heaven.

The Law of Faith is how we apply the Word in our lives, not by works we could boast about, but by the Law of God, whom we give the glory.

It's how we make formal requests to God, our authority — put them into action for a particular purpose, and then receive the promises of God, which is our right. As we apply The Law of Faith, we enter into a binding contract with the courts of Heaven and the Judge of all the earth, giving us the legal right for the promise we asked for. ***Shall not the Judge of all the earth do what is right?*** (Genesis 18:25). In the world of technology today, you may have heard, "There's an app for that." Well, there is an "app" for Faith called The Law of Faith. Apps make things more manageable, so download it today!

# Saved through Faith

Many struggle with The Law of Faith mainly because preachers say that Jesus did away with the law. They take the verse, *For by grace are ye saved **through Faith**; and that not of yourselves: it is the gift of God* (Ephesians 2:8). They put a period after saved and stop there. Yes, I agree. We are saved by grace, but it is *through* Faith. We get to grace by going *through* Faith, and as we have been learning, *through* Faith is a process that does not stop at just believing. I have seen many still "believing" but still struggling and seeing no change in their life; why? They stopped at the beginning of the process and are not experiencing the promises of God as substance and evidence in their life.

The Apostle Paul writes to the church at Ephesus and clarifies that we are saved by grace through Faith. *For it is **by grace you have been saved through Faith**, and this **not from yourselves**; it is the gift of God, **not by works**, so that **no one can boast**. For we are God's workmanship, created in Christ Jesus to do good works, which God prepared in advance as **our way of life*** (Ephesians 2:8–10). Again, he is saying we cannot boast about receiving anything from God because it is a gift that He has given us through The Law of Faith. God, in His Amazing Grace, has given us the gift of salvation; our only role is entering the legal agreement through The Law of Faith.

You can be saved if you're struggling or doubting your salvation right now. Apply the Three Aspects of Faith:

- The Word of Faith, which is God's Word, says that His grace can save you. Believe it.

- The Law of Faith, receive your salvation by entering into His legal contract and confess, I now receive my salvation! Confess "I am saved," and don't let anyone tell you differently. It's the Law!

- And now, The Spirit of Faith says, "I am now a child of God and will live the rest of my life in the joy of living by Faith and letting the Word become life in my life."

So many are struggling because they are unsure of the will of God for their life. They feel they are not worthy, not good enough, never will be good enough, are beyond hope, have done too many bad things, and have gone too far. No, no, that is not true. The grace of God has given us The Law of Faith that can change a sinner to a saint, the sick to the healed, the bound to the free, and those without purpose to find the call of God on their life.

Because there is so much teaching about Jesus doing away with the law, we've thrown out many of our legal rights to receive God's blessings. I'm sure you're now glad you have a legal right to salvation, healing, prosperity, and all the 8,630 promises of God.

What did Jesus say about the Law? **Think not** *that I am come to* **destroy the law** *or the prophets:* **I am not come to destroy**, *but to fulfill. For verily I say unto you, Till heaven and earth pass,* **one jot or one tittle shall in no wise pass from the law**, *till all be fulfilled* (Matthew 5:17).

Jesus clearly says, Don't even think that I have come to do away with the Law; many have considered it and even taught it. Jesus says I have **not** come to **destroy.** Destroy in Greek is *Katalusai—loosen, disintegrate, demolish, to halt,* *come to nought, overthrow, throw down.* Jesus goes on and says, not one jot *(iota)* or title *(letter)* will pass *(go away).* Fulfilled in Greek *Pleroo* means *partaken, published.* Thus, *Jesus* is telling us that the Law is not going away and will be published to the world. If Jesus did away with the Law, He would have said He had, but just the opposite, He said it must be published to all.

*The **law of the LORD is perfect, converting the soul**: the testimony of the LORD is sure, making wise the simple* (Psalm 19:7). Obviously, something that is perfect would not be done away with. The Law of the Lord is perfect, and it converts the soul; it changes our minds, will, and emotions and makes us wise. The Law of Faith has undoubtedly changed my life for the better. How about you?

# Through Faith, We Establish the Law

God has set a perfect law in motion for you to have a legal right to believe and receive all His promises that He put in our Bibles. Did I tell you, *"You can have, be and do everything the Bible says?"*

*Do we then make void the law **through Faith**? God forbid: yea, **we establish the law*** (Romans 3:31). We establish the law every time we operate in the Three Aspects of Faith. We demonstrate the law in another realm of our life, as seen in the Lord's prayer; Your Kingdom comes to earth like it is Heaven.

## The Law of How Faith Comes

*So then **Faith cometh by hearing** and hearing **by the word of God*** (Romans 10:17).

## The Law of Speaking

*But the righteousness which is of **Faith speaketh*** (Romans 10:6).

*That **the communication of thy Faith** may become effectual by the acknowledging of every good thing which is in you in Christ Jesus* (Philemon 1:6).

## The Law of Confession

*Let us hold fast to **the profession of our Faith** without wavering; (for he is Faithful that promised;)* (Hebrews 10:23).

*But what saith it? The word is nigh thee, even in thy mouth, and in thy heart: that is, **The Word of Faith, which we preach;** That if thou shalt **confess** with thy mouth the Lord Jesus, and shalt believe in thine heart that God hath raised him from the dead, thou shalt be saved. For with the heart, man believeth unto righteousness, and with the mouth **confession is made unto salvation*** (Romans 10:8–10). When people talk, what's in their minds will come out. If fear is in their mind, fear comes out; if doubt is in their mind, doubt comes, but if Faith is in their mind, Faith comes out. Learn to confess only what you want to manifest in your life.

## The Law Is Higher Than the Wisdom of Men

*That your Faith should not stand in the **wisdom of men**, but in **the power of God*** (1 Corinthians 2:5). I google many things because it's easy. I look at YouTube how-to videos because someone has already found a way to fix something I have a problem with. However, life offers many things that man's wisdom cannot fix. Make it a habit today to go to the one with all knowledge, wisdom, and power to fix the impossible things in your life.

## The Law of Obedience

*By whom we have received Grace and apostleship, for **obedience to the Faith** among all nations, for his name* (Romans 1:5). The Apostle Paul is saying that they have received their call to apostleship because of their obedience to the Faith. The promotion comes to you for whatever your call is through your obedience to the Faith. If God can trust you to obey the little things, He will promote you.

## The Law of the Twelve Blessings of the Tither

*Will a man rob God? Yet ye have robbed me. But ye say, Wherein have we robbed thee? In tithes and offerings. **Bring ye all the tithes into the storehouse**, that there may be meat in mine house, and prove me now herewith, saith the LORD of hosts, if **I will not open you the windows of Heaven, and pour you out a blessing**, that there **shall not be room enough to receive it*** (Malachi 3:8). When you bring your tithe, Heaven legally must open its windows and supernaturally bring blessings into your life. God invites you to prove Him in your financial situation.

## The Law of Doing Good

*As we have, therefore, opportunity, let us **do good unto all men**, especially unto them who are **of the household of Faith***

(Galatians 6:10). This law can change your outlook on life and the people you meet. Instead of thinking everybody is out to get something from you, turn it around and do good to them; God will bless you. Remember, you are blessed to be a blessing.

## The Law of Seed-Faith

***Give, and it shall be given unto you***; *good measure, pressed down, and shaken together, and running over, shall men give into your bosom. For with **the same measure** that ye mete withal, it shall be measured to you again* (Luke 6:38). I grew up as a farmer, so this law was easy to understand. I would get a bountiful harvest if I planted some little seeds in my field. If I did not plant anything well, then I received nothing.

## The Law of Worship

*And it shall be, that **whoso will not come** up of all the families of the earth unto Jerusalem to **worship the King**, the LORD of hosts, even upon them shall be **no rain*** (Zechariah 14:17). God desires our worship, and when we do, He responds with the rain of His Spirit. When you feel dry in your Faith, bring the sacrifice of praise and worship, and you will feel His remarkable presence. At my church, we start every service by entering His gates with thanksgiving and entering His courts with praise and worship. Why? We don't want a dead, dry service without healing or miracles.

## The Law of Laying on of Hands

*And these signs shall follow them that believe; In my name shall they cast out Devils; they shall speak with new tongues; They shall take up serpents; and if they drink any deadly thing, it shall not hurt them; they shall* **lay hands on the sick, and they shall recover** (Mark 16:17–18). My heart breaks to see so many people who are ill and dealing with diseases. I've learned that some illnesses result from demonic influence, and these spirits must be dealt with. Some are caused simply by the way the person talks, believing that "it" runs in the family. They need to speak in new tongues, not only in the natural but in the Spirit through prayer. Some diseases result from the substances people have put in their bodies. Regardless, God's Law can change all of this. God will legally heal us if we who believe will lay hands on the sick. I see this nearly every week in my ministry.

## The Law of Giving to Missions

***My God shall supply all your need*** *according to his riches in glory by Christ Jesus* (Philippians 4:19). The apostle is telling the church at Philippi that, because they gave to his ministry mission trips to fill the need of those in other parts of the world, God was going to bless them and meet their needs.

## The Law of Sin

*For* ***the wages of sin is death****, but the gift of God is eternal life through Jesus Christ our Lord* (Romans 6:23). The Law works positively and negatively. The legal payment for sin is death. Sin will cause our Faith and relationships to die an eternal death. Choose the gift of eternal life and not sin.

**What is sin?** *For **whatsoever is not of Faith is sin*** (Romans 14:23). Is sin smoking, drinking, spitting on the sidewalk, and kicking the cat? The best definition of sin I can give you is not a long list of bad things you should quit doing, but simply that sin means missing the mark. Sin in the *Greek is* *hamartia—to miss the mark, not share in the prize, fault, trespass. Figuratively speaking,* shooting at a target and missing the bullseye is a sin; you missed the mark and did not get the award. Today, start thinking about hitting the bullseye of the promise of God. Take careful aim with the Three Aspects of Faith; you will soon be hitting the bullseye every time.

It can be difficult, as when we try to quit sin, we focus on sin. Let me give you an example. Think of the number thirteen. Got it? Now try to forget thirteen. You can't; that's all you're thinking about. Now think about fourteen. Got it? What are you thinking about now? I hope you said fourteen. The same with trying to quit sinning; sin is all you think about. You think about quitting this and that, and then your focus is on that sin. That is why you need to go through the Process of Faith.

## The Law of Losing and Saving Our Life

***For whosoever will save his life shall lose it: but whosoever will lose his life for my sake, the same shall save it*** (Luke 9:24). When you try to save or make your own life better, you will lose it anyway. Lose your life in God, and you will have the God kind of life that He has planned for you all along.

## The Law of Living by Faith

***The just shall live by Faith*** (Galatians 3:11). Living by Faith is not thinking you don't have to work and that God will take care of you and pay your bills. Living by Faith is obeying God and legally applying everything He says about every promise. You are justified when you obey him.

## The Law of Walking by Faith

*For we **walk by Faith**, not by sight* (2 Corinthians 5:7). Walking by Faith is a lifestyle of looking at every situation or problem and seeing it as an opportunity to apply your Faith. We no longer see hurdles as problems but as opportunities for another testimony for the Glory of God.

## The Law of Devils

*And the seventy returned again with joy, saying, Lord, **even the Devils are subject unto us through thy name*** (Luke 10:17). Don't get caught up in spooky fear of the Devil or his demons. With faith, you can get them to leave. You will be defeated if you try to deal with them with your natural strength. I have seen many demons manifest in my forty years of ministry. But every time I applied The Law of Faith in Jesus's name, the Devils knew they had to submit to God and leave legally.

## And . . . All the Promises of God

*Therefore, I say unto you, **What things soever ye desire, when ye pray, believe that ye receive them, and ye shall have them*** (Mark 11:24). This verse will stretch your Faith, "whatever" you desire. Do you desire that, health, peace, joy, a better job, restored relationships, and whatever you find in the Word can be yours?

## We Have Confidence Because of the Law

*And this is **the confidence** that we have in him, that, if we ask anything **according to his will**, he heareth us: And if we know that he hear us, whatsoever we ask, we know that we have the petitions that we desired of him* (1 John 5:14–15). I like how Apostle John gives a "disclaimer" in this verse. We can have confidence if our request is "according to his will." Over the years, I have heard some outlandish prayers that were obviously not according to His will. How do we know that He hears us? Because it's according to His will. How do we know if it is His will? His will is found in your Bible and filled with promises that are according to His will. We have confidence because we see it in His Word; we believe, receive, confess, obey, and act on the promise.

I can have everything the Bible says because of the Law of Faith. I can be everything the Bible says because of the Law of Faith. I can do everything the Bible says because of the Law of Faith. I pray you will take a fresh look at your Bible and say this is such a precious book because now you know you can have, be, and do everything it says. I pray that you let the Word become life in your life.

## Questions:

- Why is it important to understand The Law of Faith?
- Have you ever considered that you were breaking The Law of Faith?
- In what areas of The Law of Faith have you been breaking the law?
- What is the "spirit of lawlessness" in the world today?
- How is living by The Law of Faith similar to living by the laws of the land?
- What is one way that you can enforce The Law of Faith?
- What area will you enforce The Law of Faith in this week?

- What are some consequences of breaking The Law of Faith?
- How many want to live by The Law of Faith?

## Prayer Focus:

- Pray that the Holy Spirit will reveal The Law of Faith to you.
- Pray that you will have ears to hear The Law of Faith.
- Pray that the Holy Spirit will reveal the areas of The Law of Faith that you're breaking.
- Pray and repent for breaking The Law of Faith.
- Pray that you will study and learn The Law of Faith.
- Pray for courage and discipline to obey The Law of Faith.
- Pray that you will be obedient to The Law of Faith.
- Pray that you will hold fast to your confession of Faith and not waver or become disobedient with your words.
- Pray that your actions will demonstrate your Faith.
- Pray that you will consciously be aware of The Law of Faith in everything and in every area of your life.
- Pray that you will live by The Law of Faith each and every time you claim one of the promises of God.
- Pray that others will understand The Law of Faith.

# CHAPTER 3
# The Just Shall Live by Faith

As we begin this chapter, please read this confession aloud: "*I can have everything the Bible says I can have, I can be everything the Bible says I can be, and I can do everything the Bible says I can do. Today I'm going to let the Word become life in my life.*"

God has unique plans for your life. He is the alpha and the omega, the beginning and the finisher of your Faith. He has started a good work in you and will Faithfully complete it.

Keep the Three Aspects of Faith in mind as you go through this chapter. Nothing will happen simply because we think about it, so the Word does not become life in our life if it does not go through the stages of the Three Aspects of Faith first.

- The first aspect of Faith is The Word of Faith (Romans 10:8–17), the message. The Word of Faith comes by hearing. No matter what you hear, you'll believe it. But spiritual hearing comes from hearing and understanding the Word of God, and that's the message.

- The second aspect of Faith is The Law of Faith found in Romans 3:27. The Law of Faith is the application of a type of contract or legal document that God has established with those who believe and act on His Word. God is a just God who won't do anything outside His law.

- The third aspect of Faith is The Spirit of Faith, the lifestyle, found in 2 Corinthians 4:13. You're in the spirit of it, caught up in it, and it begins to turn into a lifestyle.

*For therein is the righteousness of God revealed from Faith to Faith: as it is written,* **The just shall live by Faith** (Romans 1:17). The just shall live by Faith and not visit by Faith, not live by doubt six days a week and by Faith on Sunday. I see some drivers who try to live by Faith that the speed limit is 55, but to them, that means 61. When the Word says something, we need to have confidence in precisely what is said and not add or take away from it.

Let's look a little deeper into this verse, *For therein is the* **righteousness** *of God* **revealed from Faith to Faith** (Romans 1:17). Righteousness is simply being in right standing with God, in a face-to-face relationship with Him, obedient to His Word and in the process of applying His Word to your current situation. Right standing with God will be revealed from Faith to Faith; apparently, we will have some "Faith moments." Moments when we face a challenge to believe what God said or not. The Faith moment reveals if you have Faith to obey and let the Word become life in your life in this moment of challenge.

# What It Means to Live by Faith

I've had some Faith moments that have moved me to the next stage of Faith, but I've also had Faith moments that took me back a step or two. Living by Faith means we must view each Faith moment as an opportunity to move into a lifestyle of Faith. Once we see this truth, we can understand the scripture, *My brethren,* **count it all joy** *when ye fall into divers temptations;* **Knowing this***, that* **the trying of your Faith** *worketh patience.* **But let patience have her perfect work***, that ye* **may be perfect and entire, wanting nothing** (James 1:2–4). What? Do you want me to be happy about being challenged to believe in God in my test, trial, sickness, money, and worries? If we can get past the first part of the verse, count it all joy when we fall, and get to the end of the verse, to perfect, entire, wanting nothing, we can change our mindset when problems come; after all, they are only "Faith moments."

I've said many times that we are saved, being saved, and one day we will be saved. What I mean by this is that we are growing in our salvation, working out our salvation, and learning more about salvation. We are saved when we make Jesus the savior and Lord of our lives. We are being saved as we learn more of His promises and receive them from Faith-to-Faith moments, such as healing, prosperity, peace, joy, and purpose. And we will be saved when Jesus returns, and we will receive a glorified body, the completion of our salvation. I say, "Enjoy the journey," and use every opportunity to let the Word become life in your life today.

Nate, a young man in my church, testified the other day about when he got saved, and then he found out what the Bible said about the tithe, so he began to bring his tithe. He said, *"Each week, I was challenged to keep bringing the tithe in some of my Faith moments. One day, I changed my mind from bringing my tithe to becoming a tither. I started applying that, and then it was. I don't have to think about if I'm going to do it or not anymore. It's just that I've applied it and realized there are too many benefits not to do it. I mean, this thing works. God really is a good God; God said, try me, prove me, bring your tithe into the storehouse, and I'll pour out the windows of heaven and pour out blessings. I found out that what God said was true; it's a legal thing. If I tithe, it's a legal thing, and I'm going to be blessed."* I share his testimony to demonstrate Faith to Faith, moving from The Law of Faith to Living by Faith. Nate was saved, then he was saved in another area of his life, his finances, and today he is very prosperous. What area of your life would you like to be "saved" in today?

As we begin living by Faith, we accumulate some testimonies along the way on how we're being saved in new areas of our life, so we start thinking, *Well, maybe we should try some of the other things the Bible says we can have.* And then, the "Let the Word Become Life in My Life" journey becomes a wonderful phrase and concept in our daily life.

I shall live by Faith is now a lifestyle and no longer just a Sunday morning church service. If you have thought you were only holding on until Jesus comes to take you, that changes today. I love what an elderly pastor friend used to say. "I know it will be sweet in the 'sweet by and by,' but I must live in the 'nasty now and now.'" He would also say, "I need this Bible to work for me today. The good news I have for you today is, yes, this Bible will work for you today. It has for me, and it will work for you."

At this point in many people's Faith walk, they have received a few answers to prayer, so they start bombarding Heaven with all sorts of requests, but they soon become disappointed with no answers to prayer. Why? They forgot the Three Aspects of Faith, The Word of Faith—did God say it? The Law of Faith—can God legally honor it? The Spirit of Faith — does God see you living it? Then how can it possibly become life in your life? So, remember, we can have everything the Bible says we can have.

You may wonder if we're limited to what the Bible says. My friend, I have found 8,630 promises in the Bible for you and me! Most people's problem is that they do not know what those promises are and all they entail, so they receive little. The 8,630 promises will keep you busy for at least a year of constant Faith moments. Divide 8,630 by 365 days, and you get twenty-three different promises per day, with one hour to pray for them each day. Which Word do you want to become life in your life today? Start the process of the Three Aspects of Faith and watch what God will do.

## Living by Faith

Let's look at some scripture discussing the concept that the just shall live by Faith. *Now the just shall live by Faith: but **if any man draws back, my soul shall have no pleasure** in him* (Hebrews 10:38). In the Faith moment, you're either going to live by Faith, or you're going back to revert to something else. *If any man draws back, my soul shall have no pleasure*; in other words, if I see someone get going for the Lord and then, upon getting tested, they go backward, my soul doesn't have any pleasure in them. That's so sad that they were doing so well, and now they have gone backward in their Faith. If my soul is sad because of that, how much sadder must God be? He wants you to keep going, so don't throw in the towel. Keep fighting because this is a fight we can win.

So we need to keep progressing forward. Habakkuk, the prophet, points out the problem of going backward, *Behold, **his soul which is lifted up** is not upright in him: but the just shall live by his Faith* (Habakkuk 2:4). What's the problem? It's the soul; people go backward because their souls are lifted up in pride. One's soul is their mind, will, and emotions. When another thought pops up, and you believe it instead of God, your feelings get involved and lead you to a different conclusion. When this happens, you will move to act contrary to The Word of Faith based on your mind and emotions. Such a test happened even for Jesus. When Jesus was in the garden, he had to overcome his own mind, will, and emotions by putting the Word of God first. He prayed about going to the cross and said, *Not my will, but thine be done*. We, too must overcome our mind.

The Apostle Paul gives us great insight into living by Faith in writing to the Galatians, *I am **crucified** with Christ: nevertheless, **I live**; yet not I, but Christ liveth in me: and **the life which I now live** in the flesh I live by the Faith of the Son of God, who loved me and gave himself for me* (Galatians 2:20). Paul says we must crucify our life to live the actual life of Faith. Before you think the life of Faith is dying to be anything enjoyable, you don't quit living. You don't quit existing; you don't quit going to work, you don't quit going to school, you don't quit going shopping. You don't quit going on vacation — you still have life. This new life of Faith brings joy and fulfillment to everything you do in your life. This life has a higher purpose that makes you want to get out of bed to see what God will do in your day. You won't really experience this life until you live this kind of life every day instead of simply visiting this life for a couple of hours on Sunday.

Paul is saying that once I finally gave up on trying to "add" God to my life, I finally found the God kind of life that He has meant for me to live all along. I've watched people spend their entire lives trying to add more God to their lives. They try to add healing, deliverance, prosperity, purpose and a calling, etc. They try to somehow "fit" God into their busy schedule, which causes more frustration than joy. Their life becomes a percentage of themselves and a portion of God.

And as they "fit" in God, they have a mindset of "giving up things" and losing what they enjoy to be better Christians. With this mindset, you'll be so focused on what you're losing that you'll never look at what you can find in the Word that is so much better. But remember what the Word says: *For whosoever will **save his life shall lose it**: and whosoever will **lose his life for my sake shall find it*** (Matthew 16:25). I encourage you to take on the mindset of looking for what the Bible says you can have, be, and do. You will be amazed at the treasure God has in store for you.

Sometimes when learning, you can discover what something is by finding out what it's not. So it is with living by Faith.

- Expecting all the promises of God to drop out of the sky and happen (see 2 Corinthians 1:20). We must take one promise at a time and walk that promise through the Three Aspects of Faith. As we do, that promise will become life in our life.
- Expecting money to fall out of the sky. The Bible says if you don't work, you won't eat (2 Thessalonians

3:10). God blesses what you put your hand to (see Deuteronomy 28:8). God gave you the power to get wealth; He didn't give you wealth (see Deuteronomy 8:18).

- Generically saying you're just trusting God; that's religious. I always ask people what expressly God has declared that they trust him for. Trusting God is believing and doing what God said.

- Trying to be in full-time ministry. Many believe that to live by Faith truly, you must be in full-time ministry. Living by Faith is for everybody who lets the word become "life in their life." I tell young ministers that if you don't learn to live by Faith before they're in the ministry, I guarantee them 100% or 110% that they will never live by Faith in full-time ministry. Why? Because then, they will not only have problems that require their Faith, but they also will have everybody else's problems that need to be solved by Faith. If they can't figure out how to solve their problems, they will not have the answer for others.

- Saying, "I'm believing for healing." We must understand that we need a mindset change from believing for something to believing what God said about that something. Rather than believing God for healing, we must believe what God said about healing. God said to call on the elders for the prayer of Faith that will save the sick. God said believers would lay hands on the sick, and they shall recover. If you believe what God said about healing, I will see you calling on the elders, asking a believer to lay hands on you, in other words doing what God said about it, and you will have it.

## Faith Can Be Seen

Faith can be seen. The best place to start your Faith journey is with a familiar verse that sadly has been misunderstood. *Now **Faith is the substance** of things hoped for, **the evidence** of things not seen* (Hebrews 11:1). Look at this verse carefully to see what it says. Faith can be seen by the substance and evidence. Faith is a substance that can be touched, felt, and experienced. Evidence can also be seen in the natural; just like in a court of law, evidence is presented as proof of its existence, which others can see to prove the case. If there is no substance or evidence, then the rest of the verse explains that you are still in the stage of the things hoped for that are not seen yet. We must determine if we are in the Faith stage or in the hope stage; either one is excellent. The scripture says, *Hope maketh us not ashamed* (Romans 5:5). Thank God you are in the hope stage; that is better than not having hope at all for a promise of God. The problem arises when a person confuses the hope stage with the Faith stage. Be honest; you are in the hope stage if you don't have Faith yet, meaning you don't have the evidence. Please don't stop at the hope stage; go back through the Three Aspects of Faith until your thinking manifests into the type of Faith that can be proved and seen with evidence.

Faith is the evidence of things not seen. It's not just talking but a demonstration. Jesus didn't talk about Faith; he demonstrated Faith. He said, "God is the God that healeth thee," and then demonstrated it. Jesus didn't pray for people and hoped to God that they would recover in six months. When he prayed for a blind person, their eyes opened — now that's the substance. Do you understand the difference between hope and substance? I hear people who are sick saying, "I am healed." The reality is if they were healed, they would not be saying they were healed; they would be healed — and everyone could see the evidence.

There is another verse that illustrates that Faith can be seen: *And this gospel of the kingdom shall be **preached** in all the world for **a witness** unto all nations* (Matthew 24:14). Here we see two things, preaching and a witness. The preaching is The Word of Faith, the message, the promises of God. Next, there is the witness or demonstration of what is being preached. Again, like in a court of law, evidence is presented so people can see and hear witnesses that saw it happen. The preaching of the gospel loses its power when there is no witness or demonstration. People will believe the Word that is being preached when they see the witness and evidence. You are learning how to let the Word become life in your life. That means your life will be the sermon and the witness.

James tells us that Faith can be seen in his life. *Yea, a man may say, Thou hast Faith, and I have works: shew me thy Faith without thy works, and **I will shew thee my Faith by my works**. Thou believest that there is one God; thou doest well: the devils also believe and tremble. But wilt thou know, O vain man, that **Faith without works is dead**?* (James 2:18–20).

The most impressive example of Faith is seen in Mark 2:3–11. Some men take a man who is sick with palsy to the meeting that Jesus is ministering in. They can't get in the door because of the crowd, so they take him up on his bed on the roof, tear the roof off the building, and let him down through the roof in front of Jesus and the crowd. I don't know if they said,

Lord Jesus, please heal this man. I don't know if they had an uplifted hand with a silent prayer request. I don't know if somebody spoke anything whatsoever. But Jesus didn't need to hear them say anything. He saw their Faith when he saw them tear the roof apart and lower the man down. He said unto the sick of the palsy, "Son be of good cheer. Your sins are forgiven and take up your bed and walk" (Mark 2:9).

Faith can also be perceived as demonstrated by the Apostle Paul in Acts. *The same heard Paul speak who steadfastly beholding him, and* **perceiving that he had Faith to be healed**, *Said with a loud voice, Stand upright on thy feet. And he leaped and walked* (Acts 14:9–10). Paul was preaching along, and this man kept looking at him, and Paul perceived he had Faith to be healed. As preachers, you should know when someone has Faith to be healed. When people come to the altar, I see if they have Faith to be healed or if I will have to talk to them for a while and build their Faith until they're ready to receive. You can also perceive when people don't have Faith to be healed.

Can Faith be seen in your life? ***Examine yourselves, whether ye be in the Faith;*** *prove your own selves Know ye, not your own selves, how that Jesus Christ is in you* (2 Corinthians 13:5). Examine yourself to see how many times you're in the Faith or how many times you're in doubt. If you're not satisfied with how many times you can see Faith, it's as simple as a decision to let the Word become life in your life in more areas of your life.

I remember a time when I was preaching to a group of about a thousand people in Argentina. I was speaking with an interpreter, so I would preach a phrase, and he would then interpret it into Spanish, then back and forth throughout the message. As I spoke, I asked a man to come forward because I had a word for him. He came forward, and I said, "God wants to heal your back. Bend over and touch your toes." My interpreter asked me in English, "Are you sure you know what you're doing?" I was surprised he asked this as we have moved in healing together many times before. Anyway, I said, "Yes, of course." and he proceeded to translate it into Spanish. The man looked a little puzzled for a moment and then bent over and touched his toes. The crowd went wild, cheering and praising God, and many started coming to the altar to get saved. I thought this was ridiculous. So, what was the big deal? I thought the man had simply received healing in his back until I found out why the interpreter had asked me if I knew what I was doing. The man had had four vertebrae welded together, and it was impossible for him to bend over, and the crowd knew this about this man. The group knew this was not simply a healing; they knew it was a miracle. The group saw the man's Faith even to try to bend over, and then they saw Faith, substance, evidence, and a manifestation of the Word of God. I joked with my pastor friend, the interpreter, afterward that I was glad I did not know his back was welded together — I'm not sure how good my Faith would have been to call it out if I had known!

I pray that your Faith will be seen as a witness and demonstration of the Kingdom of God as you let this Word become life in your life.

## Questions:

- Why is it important to "live" by Faith?
- Can anyone live by Faith?
- Is it more challenging to live by Faith than by the senses?
- Why are you commanded to live by Faith?
- What is a simple definition of living by Faith?
- What is living by Faith not?
- What is the biggest hindrance to living by Faith?
- How is righteousness revealed by those who live by Faith?
- How does living by Faith bring the good life or the life that deserves the name of life?
- How can Faith be seen?
- How can Faith be perceived?
- Give an example of when you saw Faith.
- Give an example of when you perceived Faith.
- How can Faith be seen in your life?

## Prayer Focus:

- Pray that you will see and recognize the Three Aspects of Faith.
- Pray that you will see the three aspects are saved, being saved, and will be saved.
- Pray that the Lord reveals where you live in the Three Aspects of Faith.

- Pray that you will let the Faith moments in your life move you from Faith to Faith.
- Pray that you will not be drawn back to your old life in the seven mountains of influence.
- Pray that the Lord will reveal the message your old life is still preaching.
- Pray that you will understand what the saving of the soul really means.
- Pray that you will understand what being crucified with Christ has to do with genuinely being born again and have become a new creature, and all the old ways have passed away.
- Pray that you will examine yourself to see if you are in the Faith with evidence others can see.
- Pray that the Lord will reveal to you when you are only trying to add God to your life and not making Him your life.
- Pray that you will make living by Faith a daily priority.
- Pray that your life will be a testimony as you live and demonstrate The Word of Faith operating in your life.
- Pray that you will see and recognize people who have Faith.
- Pray that you will become more sensitive and be able to perceive when people have Faith.
- Pray that the Holy Spirit will guard your lips and help you to keep your confessions aligned with the Word.
- Pray that your life will be a testimony as you live and demonstrate The Word of Faith operating in your life.

# CHAPTER 4

# Five Levels of Faith

As we begin this chapter, please read this confession aloud: "*I can have everything the Bible says I can have, I can be everything the Bible says I can be, and I can do everything the Bible says I can do. Today I'm going to let the Word become life in my life.*"

The scriptures reveal that Five Levels of Faith are available for us to walk in. You are about to discover, as we go through each level, why your Faith has worked in some areas of your life and why it has not worked in other areas of your life. I promise you will find your level and the blessing for each. Please don't skip to level five as they are progressive and bring specific blessings for each level.

## Level One — The Measure of Faith

*For I say, through the grace given unto me, to every man that is among you, not to think of himself more highly than he ought to think, but to think soberly, according as God hath dealt to every man **the measure of Faith*** (Romans 12:3). This is the foundation verse we will call level one.

God has dealt to every man The Measure of Faith, so you have Faith right now. God has given you a portion, a share — a limited portion — and He wants you to use what you have, and He will give you more. This level is like a small down payment; you can gain, multiply, and increase in Faith as you use it. The good news is that you are already at level one.

Let's turn to the scriptures or to the "Faith chapter", as some would call it. *But without Faith, it is impossible to **please him**: for he that cometh to God must **believe that he is**, and that he is a **rewarder of them that diligently seek him*** (Hebrews 11:6). We are already blessed in this first level of Faith because we can believe, seek, and please Him. You are already pleasing God by seeking Him as you study The Five Levels of Faith today. Many have said, "Well, I believe in God," but I tell them we don't stop there; that's not the end of the story. This verse says that God will reward you for diligently seeking Him more and more each day.

James addresses The Measure of Faith, *Yea, a man may say, Thou hast Faith, and I have works: shew me thy Faith without thy works, and **I will shew thee my Faith by my works**. **Thou believest that there is one God; thou doest well: the devils also believe and tremble**. But wilt thou know, O vain man, that **Faith without works is dead**?* (James 2:18–20). Everybody has been given this level of Faith. Everyone believes there's a God somewhere, even if they may not know his name. Some say they don't believe in God but spend a lot of time and effort trying to prove that He whom they do not believe in does not exist — even the devils believe in God and tremble (James 2:19). But without a relationship, they will be dead and not produce. I have heard some say they prayed to the man upstairs; you can tell they don't have a relationship with Him because, by their vocabulary, they are not showing their Faith through works or obedience.

## Level Two — No Faith

Let's move on to level two. Wait a minute. Level two is No Faith? Sometimes we go backward before we go forward. *They provoked him to jealousy with strange gods, with abominations provoked they him to anger. They sacrificed unto devils, not to God; to gods whom they knew not, to new gods that came newly up, whom your fathers feared not. And he said, I will hide my face from them, I will see what their end shall be: for they are a very froward generation, children in whom there is **no Faith*** (Deuteronomy 32:16–17).

We find ourselves at the second level of Faith, No Faith. Did I mention that sometimes we go backward instead of forward? We start heading toward God, then we run into a slight problem and run for the hills; we go after other gods and the world system to solve our problem. We have a pity party, invite others to our party, try entertainment, drugs, medication, and the list of what we return to. God says, They do not believe me; they have No Faith in me right now, so I will wait to see how those other solutions will work out. It won't be long before we discover that the world's system does not solve our problem and often worsens it. Have you experienced graduating to level two in your Faith a few times in your life? Take a deep breath, laugh at yourself, and be glad you are at least biblical by being at level two. Are you ready to move on to level three?

# Level Three — Little Faith

Jesus speaks about the third level of Faith. *But when ye pray, use not vain repetitions, as the heathen do: for they think that they shall be heard for their much speaking. Be not ye, therefore, like unto them: for your Father knoweth what things ye have need of before ye ask him* (Matthew 6:7–8). We have just found out we were at level two, with No Faith, so what do we do? Pray! God has been waiting for us to get tired of being at level two and knew our next step would be to pray! Jesus continues. *Wherefore, if God so clothe the grass of the field, which today is, and tomorrow is cast into the oven, shall he not much more clothe you, O ye **of little Faith?*** (Matthew 6:30). As soon as we leave level two of No Faith and begin praying, we reach level three. We have Faith again and realize our Heavenly Father loves us, knows our needs, and is ready to answer our prayers.

When we are in Little Faith, Jesus tells us we use vain repetitions. I've heard people pray the same prayer every time they pray. They may have three different versions of it, but it's essentially the same. Our Father desires us to be personal in our prayers. He knows our needs, so communicate with Him and praise Him for the answer. You will be surprised at what you can do with Little Faith.

We find the disciples with Little Faith. *And when he was entered into a ship, his disciples followed him. And, behold, there arose a great tempest in the sea, insomuch that the ship was covered with the waves: but he was asleep. And his disciples came to him, and awoke him, saying, **Lord, save us**: we perish. And he saith unto them, Why are ye fearful, O ye of **little Faith**? Then he arose and rebuked the winds and the* *sea, and there was a great calm.* (Matthew 8:23–26). Jesus demonstrates to them what Little Faith can do — calm the storm.

Here we see the disciples praying a little Faith in the vain repetition of prayer: Lord, please save us. Jesus rebukes the storm and tells them they are in Little Faith, implying they could have prayed a prayer that would stop the storm. Why couldn't they? Because they had Little Faith, that's the level they were at. They had Little Faith and only believed Jesus could save them. If you are at Little Faith, rejoice; Little Faith can save you.

Jesus gives us another example of Little Faith, *And when his disciples were come to the other side, they had forgotten to take bread. Then Jesus said unto them, Take heed and beware of the leaven of the Pharisees and of the Sadducees. And they reasoned among themselves, saying, It is because we have taken no bread. When Jesus perceived, he said unto them,* ***O ye of little Faith****, why reason ye among yourselves, because ye have brought no bread? Do ye not yet understand, neither remember the five loaves of the five thousand, and how many baskets ye took up? Neither the seven loaves of the four thousand and how many baskets ye took up? How is it that ye do not understand that I spake it not to you concerning bread, that ye should beware of the leaven of the Pharisees and of the Sadducees?* (Matthew 16:5–11). This verse should encourage you that the disciples were accomplishing many things while still operating in Little Faith.

The disciples forgot to take some bread and found themselves in Little Faith. To clarify, Jesus was not talking about natural bread but was teaching about the wrong doctrine or leaven of the Pharisees. If we have Little Faith, we won't be prepared when we hear the false doctrine. When we hear false doctrine, it can cause our Faith to stumble and doubt God's Word. Be careful who you listen to; are they preaching The Word of Faith?

Noah prepared, and Joseph stored up for seven years, so it would be wise to use our Faith in advance. If we fail to prepare, we could find ourselves with Little Faith and asking for help.

Let's look at one more example of Little Faith: *But straightway Jesus spake unto them, saying, Be of good cheer; it is I;* **be not afraid**. *And Peter answered him and said, Lord, if it be thou, bid me come unto thee on the water. And he said, Come. And* **when Peter was come down out of the ship, he walked on the water to go to Jesus. But when he saw the wind boisterous, he was afraid; and beginning to sink, he cried, saying, Lord, save me.** *And immediately Jesus stretched forth his hand, and caught him, and said unto him,* **O thou of little Faith**, *wherefore didst thou doubt?* (Matthew 14:27–31). Jesus encouraged Peter to move to another level of Faith by stepping out of the boat and walking on water. Peter took three steps into the next level of Faith, but as soon as he looked at the circumstances around him, he returned to Little Faith and cried, "Lord save me!" I encourage you to step out of your boat into the next level of Faith. Even if the circumstances overwhelm you, you can still be confident that your Little Faith will save you.

# Level Four — Great Faith

We find how Great Faith operates in this portion of scripture. *And when Jesus was entered into Capernaum, there came unto him a centurion, beseeching him, And saying, Lord, my servant lieth at home sick of the palsy, grievously tormented. And Jesus saith unto him, I will come and heal him. The centurion answered and said, Lord, I am not worthy that thou shouldest come under my roof: but speak the word only, and my servant shall be healed. For I am a man under authority, having soldiers under me: and I say to this man, Go, and he goeth; and to another, Come, and he cometh; and to my servant, Do this, and he doeth it. When Jesus heard it, he marveled, and said to them that followed, Verily I say unto you, I have not found so* **great Faith**, *no, not in Israel* (Matthew 8:5–10). The centurion demonstrates Great Faith because he is coming to Jesus for someone other than himself. When we move past Faith for ourselves and desire to use our Faith for someone else, we move into level four, which Jesus calls Great Faith. Jesus responds and says he will come and heal him, but then the centurion says something that impresses Jesus, "Just speak the Word only, and my servant will be healed." Jesus had been trying to get his disciples to speak to the storm, talk to provision, and encourage them to step into this next level of Faith, kingdom authority. Jesus explains that the centurion understands kingdom authority. When we understand the principle of submission and authority, we will begin to take God's Word, speak His Word to our circumstances, and see them change. Great Faith speaks to the sickness, the disease, and the storm knowing that God's word is the final authority in the situation and the problem has to submit to His authority. Remember, it is The Law of Faith, and God honors His Law.

We find one more example of Great Faith. *And, behold,* **a woman of Canaan** *came out of the same coasts, and cried unto him, saying, Have mercy on me, O Lord, thou Son of David; my daughter is grievously vexed with a devil. But he answered her, not a word. And his disciples came and besought him, saying, Send her away; for she crieth after us. But he answered and said, I am not sent but unto the lost sheep of the house of Israel. Then came she and worshipped him, saying, Lord, help me. But he answered and said, It is not meet to take the children's bread and to cast it to dogs. And she said, Truth, Lord: yet the dogs eat of the* **crumbs which fall from their masters' table**. *Then Jesus answered and said unto her,* **O woman, great is thy Faith***: be it unto thee even as thou wilt.* **And her daughter was made whole from that very hour** (Matthew 15:22–28). Here we find a woman from Cana that the Jews considered to be a pagan dog and less than worthy to receive from God. Have people made you feel like a dog and a little unworthy because you're not in the right crowd, born on the other side of the tracks, and not as privileged? Don't let people's opinions stop you from entering Great Faith today!

This lady comes worshiping Jesus and says, "Lord help me in my Little Faith." She understood that Jesus was not yet sent to the gentiles, but she said even the dogs eat the crumbs from the master's table and that one crumb from Heaven, one word from God, can change my life. Jesus responds and calls her a woman of Great Faith. Her daughter was healed that very hour. We can see from this example that when we step into Great Faith, the answer comes immediately.

I remember once in a church service when I had a Word of Knowledge that someone in the congregation had had pain in their thumb for years. A young man responded that he did. I prayed for him, and he was instantly healed of an injury he had dealt with for years. That one Word from God changed his thumb and his entire life; he is now a minister in my church and praying for others. No matter where you're at, you can act in Faith, and no matter who you are, you can act in Faith today.

# Where Are You At?

What you receive will be determined by what level of Faith you're at. Before we get to level five, I want to give you a checklist, so you can assess where you're at.

## According to Your Faith

*And when he was come into the house, the blind men came to him: and Jesus saith unto them,* **Believe ye that I am able to do this?** *They said unto him, Yea, Lord. Then touched he their eyes, saying,* **According to your Faith** *be it unto you* (Matthew 9:28–29). Jesus is asking them if they believe He is able to heal them. He is determining what level of Faith they're at. He discovers they are at level three, and He heals them. Again, any level of Faith is fantastic and will bring different promises of God into your life.

## Faith as Seed

*Then came the disciples to Jesus apart, and said, Why could not we cast him out? And Jesus said unto them, Because of your unbelief: for verily I say unto you,* **If ye have Faith as a grain of mustard seed***, ye shall* **say unto this mountain***, Remove hence to yonder place; and it shall remove, and nothing shall be impossible unto you. Howbeit, this kind goeth not out but* *by prayer and fasting* (Matthew 17:19–21). Jesus explains to his disciples that they could not cast out devils because they were not at the level of Great Faith, which requires speaking to the issue, as we learned in the section on Great Faith. Also, it will take fasting or a time of preparation in intimate prayer with the Father before the encounter. Speaking to a problem is compared with sowing a seed of the Word of God that will grow into a complete harvest. Nothing is impossible when we operate in Great Faith.

## Increase Your Faith

*And the apostles said unto the Lord,* ***Increase our Faith****. And the Lord said, If ye had Faith as a grain of mustard seed, ye might say unto this sycamine tree, Be thou plucked up by the root, and be thou planted in the sea; and it should obey you* (Luke 17:5–6). Jesus tells them how to increase their Faith and step into the level of Great Faith by learning to speak to the situations and not just asking Jesus to fix them for them, which we learned was the level of Little Faith. I can't help but say, "Let the Word become life in your life," and begin speaking His Word and move to Great Faith that pleases God.

## Faith to Faith

*For therein is the righteousness of God revealed from* ***Faith to Faith*** *as it is written that just shall live by Faith* (Romans 1:17). Righteousness is better understood as being in right standing with God. Obviously, when we are in the No Faith level, we are not in right standing or standing face-to-face with God. The time we spend face-to-face with God will be revealed from one level of Faith to the next. Whatever level of Faith we're at, there will be tests and trials to turn us away, but in these times, we turn and face God again and move to a higher level of Faith. I know no one enjoys the tests, but that is when we have to exercise our Faith. So, enjoy the journey and continue to the next level of Faith.

## Level Five — Full of Faith

Level five is revealed in this scripture: *And **the word of God increased**, and the number of **the disciples multiplied** in Jerusalem greatly, and a great company of **the priests were obedient to the Faith**. And **Stephen, full of Faith** and power, **did great wonders and miracles among the people*** (Acts 6:7–8). As the number of disciples increased, twelve realized they needed help ministering to the daily food distribution. They said they could not leave preaching the Word of God to attend to serving at tables, so they called deacons to help them. The Word of God increased and spread into the city as they began delegating these responsibilities. After many heard and saw this demonstration of Faith, the number of disciples multiplied. What I love about this verse is that Stephen is a deacon, not an apostle but a servant, who did great wonders and miracles among the people. You do not have to be an apostle or pastor to walk Full of Faith and see wonders and miracles; it is for anyone who will press into it.

We read of Barnabas, another man who was Full of Faith. *For he was a good man and **full of the Holy Ghost and of Faith: and many people were added unto the Lord*** (Acts 11:24).

As you begin to walk in level five, Full of Faith, you can expect that those you talk to will be added to the church, and they will increase in their levels of Faith. You can expect miracles to begin to happen in your life.

## Progress Isn't a Straight Line

Every day, you need to ask yourself what level of Faith you're at now. I must confess there were times when I went from Full of Faith to No Faith overnight.

One of my ministers was helping put shingles on my roof. I turned to him and said, "You know this is a steep roof, and I believe backsliding is not the answer." It's easy to slide back in your Faith when you let your guard down. Sometimes we get tired of fighting the fight of Faith and want a break.

When the test comes, you might find yourself saying where's my Faith? I don't know where it is. I had it a little while ago. I don't know what I've done with it; I think I left it at church. I left my Faith at church on Sunday and needed it Tuesday afternoon. Where's your Faith?

Let's pray like the disciples. Lord, increase our Faith (Luke 17:5). You probably won't wake up in the morning with a full tank of Faith because you used your Faith the day before. You went to the gas station and filled up once, but you must return and fill up again. The same with Faith. Faith comes by hearing and hearing by the Word of God. How much time you spend reading, praying, and hearing the word of God will determine how much Faith is in your tank. Little, Great, or Full of Faith. How much Faith do you want to put in your tank today, at least enough to get you through? Why not add a little extra to give somebody else a ride on your Faith?

I trust that no matter where you're at in the different levels of Faith throughout your week, there's no condemnation; recognize it and receive the blessings of your level of Faith.

I pray that this word will become life in your life, whatever level of Faith you're at; I'm excited for you and with you, and I encourage you to move forward this week in Jesus' name, amen!

## Questions:

- What are The Five Levels of Faith?
- Why does the first level of Faith not guarantee salvation in any area of your life?
- What level of Faith do you find yourself in most of the time?
- Do you recognize what keeps you at the level of Faith you're currently in? What is it?
- What must you change to advance to the next level of Faith?
- Why must the Three Aspects of Faith be applied to each level of Faith to operate at that level?
- What level of Faith do you desire to advance to this year?
- What is one way you can increase your Faith?

## Prayer Focus:

- Pray that the Holy Spirit will reveal what level of Faith you are walking in.
- Pray that you will activate your Faith regardless of what level of Faith you are walking in.
- Pray the disciples' prayer, "Lord, Increase Our Faith."

- Pray that you will take every opportunity to hear The Word of Faith (church, YouTube, Preaching, etc.) so you can increase your Faith.
- Pray for the desire to "Live by Faith."
- Pray for boldness to tell people the truth about where they are concerning their level of Faith.
- Pray that you will use your Faith in every circumstance, problem, and challenge that comes your way.
- Pray that you will graduate from one level of Faith to another this year.
- Pray that you will use your Faith as a seed that can change anything.
- Pray that you will increase from Faith to Faith until you are Full of Faith so you can see miracles, disciples, and souls added to the church.

# CHAPTER 5

# The Process of Faith

As we begin this chapter, please read this confession aloud: "*I can have everything the Bible says I can have, I can be everything the Bible says I can be, and I can do everything the Bible says I can do. Today I'm going to let the Word become life in my life.*"

The Process of Faith works through the Three Aspects of Faith and The Five Levels of Faith.

In chapter 1, we learned of the Three Aspects of Faith

    The Word of Faith—The Message

    The Law of Faith—The Application

    The Spirit of Faith—The Lifestyle

In chapter 4, we learned of The Five Levels of Faith

    The Measure of Faith

    No Faith

    Little Faith

    Great Faith

    Full of Faith

These aspects and levels appear as you go through the Process of Faith.

## The Six Steps in the Process of Faith

Everything has a process; it doesn't just happen. So it is, too, with the Process of Faith. As we go through the Process of Faith, I will give you some practical tips, techniques, and tools, and I'll include which Aspect of Faith and Level of Faith coincides with each step in the process.

- Hear
- Believe
- Receive
- Confess
- Obey
- Act

### Step One — Hear

*So, then* **Faith cometh by <u>hearing</u> and <u>hearing by the word</u>** *of God* (Romans 10:17). The Process of Faith begins with hearing the Word of God. You can't believe it until you listen to what God says about a promise. Hearing is the first Aspect of Faith — *The Word of Faith* — and the first Level of Faith — *The Measure of Faith*. When we hear, we will either believe or doubt the Word. If we hear, we can move on in the process; however, if we doubt, we will find ourselves at the second Level of Faith: No Faith. *For unto us was the gospel preached, as well as unto them: but the word preached did not profit them, not being mixed with Faith in them that heard it* (Hebrews 4:2). Those at this level heard the Word but didn't trust what God said. Let me give this example: Look at a chair near you. Do you believe that chair exists? Do you believe that chair will hold you up? But why is that chair not holding you up? Because you're not sitting in it. You can believe what Jesus said, but if you don't sit in it — trust it completely — it will not hold you up.

I am reminded of a story my cousin told me. Her daughter was out on the sidewalk drawing chalk marks, and she called out to her. "Dolores, it's time to come in and eat. Dolores, I said it's time to come in and eat. Dolores, do you hear me?"

Dolores responded, "No, Mommy, I can't hear you."

I wonder how often Jesus calls us to come in and partake of the Word of Life, and we respond, "No, Jesus, I can't hear you." Jesus said, **He that hath ears to hear, <u>let him hear</u>** (Matthew 11:15). Not everyone with ears has ears to hear; not everyone that's listened to the word has heard it enough to begin acting on it.

*For the invisible things of him from* **the creation of the world are clearly seen**, *being* **understood** *by the things that are made, even His eternal power and Godhead; so that* **they are without excuse** (Romans 1:20–22). You are without excuse you heard, but you're acting like you didn't hear; you're going back to No Faith.

Jesus tells a story in Luke 14 about a man who made a great supper and invited many, but everyone began to come up with excuses for why they could not come. They had purchased some new tools, had just married, or had family responsibilities. The man told his servants to go to the streets and find the poor, the maimed, and the blind and compel them to come to his supper. Jesus then made this profound statement: If any man hates not his father, mother, wife, children, brethren, sister, and his own life, he cannot be my disciple. Jesus is simply saying that family members may be the very ones that hinder you from being dedicated to the Lord. Why? Because you love them so much, not realizing coming to Jesus will be the best thing you can do for your family. Beware, the enemy will often use those closest to you to keep you from God.

If we want to proceed in the Process of Faith, we may have to shake the dust off from those who don't receive us. *And whosoever shall not receive you, nor hear your words, when ye depart out of that house or city, shake off the dust of your feet* (Matthew 10:14). Some will not understand your newfound Faith because it is foolishness to them. *For the preaching of the cross is to them that perish foolishness; but unto us which are saved, it is the power of God* (1 Corinthians 1:18).

## Step Two — Believe

*For **I am not ashamed of the gospel of Christ**: for it is **the power of God unto salvation** to **every one that believeth**; to the Jew first, and also to the Greek. For therein is the righteousness of God revealed **from Faith to Faith**: as it is written, The just shall live by Faith* (Romans 1:16). Believing is the second step in the Process of Faith, and as we discovered, many things will try to stop us, and we will have to fight to believe. To believe is still the first Aspect of Faith—*The Word of Faith* but now you have moved past Level Two — *No Faith* — and you're in the third Level of Faith—*Little Faith*. When we truly believe the power of God goes into operation and things start getting exciting.

*For this cause also thank we God without ceasing, because, when ye received the word of God which ye heard of us, ye received it not as the word of men, but as it is in truth, the word of God, which **effectually worketh also in you that believe*** (1 Thessalonians 2:13). When we believe the Word of God as truth above all truth, the Word begins to work effectively in our life. We used to sing: "The Word is working mightily in me, no matter what the circumstances or what I feel or see the Word is working mightily in me."

## Step Three — Receive

*Therefore, I say unto you, What things soever ye desire, when ye pray, **believe that ye receive** them, and **ye shall have them*** (Mark 11:24). Receiving is the third step in the Process of Faith. We now move into the second Aspect of Faith — *The Law of Faith* — the application — and the third Level of Faith — *Little Faith*, which we have found to bring many blessings into our life. As we move from believing to receiving, we now receive the blessings and the life we desired when we started believing. In the receiving step, we apply The Law of Faith; we know we have a legal contract with God and that he will back it up in the courts of Heaven. We are no longer trying and fighting to believe; we say thank you, Lord, for the gift you are giving me. Remember, you can have everything the Bible says you can have.

We find a perfect example of receiving in Matthew. *Behold, a woman, which was diseased with an issue of blood twelve years, came behind him and touched the hem of his garment: For she said within herself, **If I may but touch his garment, I shall be whole*** (Matthew 9:20). Go ahead and touch, grab ahold of, and receive your promise.

## Step Four — Confess

*We having the same **spirit of Faith**, according as it is written, **I believed**, and therefore **have I spoken**; we also believe, and **therefore speak*** (2 Corinthians 4:13). Confessing is the fourth step in the Process of Faith. In this step, we move to the third Aspect of Faith—The Spirit of Faith, Lifestyle. We also move to the fourth Level of Faith—Great Faith. This step in the process moves our Faith from our heads into our mouths. Thoughts have power, but words have greater power. Thoughts may change us, but the words of our mouths have the power to change things.

*The **centurion answered and said, Lord**, I am not worthy that thou shouldest come under my roof: **but speak the word only, and my servant shall be healed**. For **I am a man under authority**, having soldiers under me: and I say to this man, Go, and he goeth; and to another, Come, and he cometh; and to my servant, Do this, and he doeth it. **When Jesus heard it, he marveled, and said to them that followed, Verily I say unto you, I have not found so GREAT FAITH, no, not in Israel*** (Matthew 8:8–10). This verse is loaded with wisdom for confession. First, speak the word only; don't confess the already obvious problem, but confess the solution that will change the situation. Your confession must be spoken with authority. God has given you the authority to speak His Word and finds pleasure when you do. Confession moves you from Little Faith to Great Faith.

*But the righteousness, which is of **Faith speaketh** on this wise, But what saith it? The word is nigh thee, even in thy mouth, and in thy heart: that is, **The Word of Faith, which we preach;** That **if thou shalt confess with thy mouth** the*

*Lord Jesus, and shalt <u>**believe in thine heart**</u> that God hath raised him from the dead, thou shalt be saved.* *For with the heart, man believeth unto righteousness; and with the mouth, <u>**confession is made unto salvation**</u>* (Romans 10:6–10). This verse confirms the transition from the belief steps to the confession step. We believe in our hearts, but confession brings salvation. A simple example would be that you believe your dog will come to you, but he won't until you say, "Come here, Fido!"

*Let us **hold fast** to **the profession of our Faith** without wavering; (for he is faithful that promised)* (Hebrews 10:23). It is easy to slip back to just believing. If you remember my example with a fluid buildup in my cheek, my wife asked me, "What are you doing about it?" Well, I had slipped back into just believing, but, as soon as I spoke to it, the fluid dissipated immediately. Hold on to your confession, keep speaking Faith, and you will have what you believe. Words, and especially the Words of God, are powerful.

## Step Five — Obey

*Know ye not, that to whom ye **yield yourselves servants to obey**, his servants ye are to whom **ye obey**, whether of sin unto death or of **obedience unto righteousness?*** (Romans 6:16). Obeying is the fifth step in the Process of Faith. We continue developing the third Aspect of Faith, our Lifestyle of Faith. We are also continuing to develop the fourth Level of Faith and finding we can have Great Faith in many other areas of our life.

*Casting down imaginations, and every high thing that exalteth itself against the knowledge of God, and **bringing*** *into captivity every thought to the obedience of Christ; And having in a readiness to revenge all disobedience, when your obedience is fulfilled* (2 Corinthians 10:5). As we hear and believe more of God's promises, we begin to cast down thoughts contrary to His Word. When we realize these thoughts can steal the blessings of God from us, we begin to hate these lies, cast them down, and replace them with the Word of God. Each time we change our minds and choose to obey, we can move into Great Faith for more and more of His promises. Take one hour of your day and see how many thoughts go through your head. You will be amazed and probably overwhelmed by how many ridiculous thoughts come to drown out God's Word. To obey him, you must hear his Word. Remember, this is a process, so change a few thoughts daily into what God says about it. What are we doing? We are letting the Word become life in our life. We are bringing every thought to the obedience of Christ and His Word. Each time you do, you grow in Faith.

## Step Six — Act

*And the saying pleased the whole multitude: and they chose Stephen,* **a man FULL OF FAITH** *and of the Holy Ghost, and Philip, and Prochorus, and Nicanor, and Timon, and Parmenas, and Nicolas a proselyte of Antioch: Whom they set before the apostles: and when they had prayed, they laid their hands on them. And* **the word of God increased**, *and the number of the* **disciples multiplied** *in Jerusalem greatly, and a great company of* **the priests were obedient to the Faith**. *And Stephen,* **full of Faith and power, did great wonders and miracles** *among the people* (Acts 6:5–8). We have reached step six, the last step in the Process of Faith. We are at the third and final Aspect of Faith—The Spirit of Faith,

The Lifestyle. We have reached the fifth and final Level of Faith—Full of Faith.

The fun begins when the action happens because you've stepped into what God has planned all along for your life. You are Full of Faith, the Word of God spreads to your community, disciples are multiplied, pastors and priests in your city become obedient to the Faith, and signs, wonders, and miracles will happen. The process to get there may have been painful sometimes, but it was well worth it.

*What doth it profit, my brethren, though a man says he **hath Faith** and have **not works**? Can Faith save him? Even so, **Faith, if it hath not works, is dead, being alone**. Yea, a man may say, Thou hast Faith, and I have works: shew me thy Faith without thy works, and I **will shew thee my Faith by my works**. For as the body without the spirit is dead, so **Faith without works is dead also*** (James 2:14–18, 26). Action should become a lifestyle. Being full of Faith and action is not just for Sunday at church anymore; it has become life in your life. Your new job is to work in the Kingdom daily, showing and demonstrating your Faith wherever you go. Where do you perform this new job? At the grocery store, McDonald's, Taco Bell, your favorite restaurant, Walmart, a high school, a gas station, and wherever you find yourself during your day. *And he said unto them, **Go ye into all the world**, and **preach the gospel to every creature**. And they went forth, and preached everywhere, the Lord working with them, and confirming the word with signs following. Amen* (Mark 16:15–20).

# A Word of Wisdom to Keep Your Momentum

Don't grow weary but keep following those that you know have Faith and evidence of the promises working in their lives. *That ye be not slothful, but **followers of them who through Faith and patience inherit the promises*** (Hebrews 6:12).

We all need leadership in our lives, but follow only those who preach the Word that builds your Faith. *Remember them which have the rule over you, who have spoken unto you the **word of God**: **whose Faith follow**, considering the end of their conversation* (Hebrews 13:7).

Let the Word become life in your life.

# Questions:

- What are the steps in the Process of Faith?
- Will Faith work if the process is out of order?
- What part of the Process of Faith is more difficult for you?
- Can the Process of Faith work in any area of your life?
- What hinders you the most in the Process of Faith?
- Can the Process of Faith be interrupted?
- Can the Process of Faith become "second nature?"

## Prayer Focus:

- Pray that the Holy Spirit will reveal the Process of Faith and where you are in the process.

- Pray for understanding where you are in the Three Aspects and the Levels of Faith as you go through the Process of Faith.

- Pray that you will have ears to hear The Word of Faith.

- Pray that you will believe the Word of God is the final authority in every area of your life.

- Pray that you will receive the Word of Promise and have it.

- Pray that you will boldly confess the Word, releasing the power of God into your circumstances.

- Pray for the courage to obey the Word.

- Pray that you will use your Faith in every circumstance, problem, and challenge that comes your way.

- Pray that you will put action to your Faith.

- Pray that your actions will demonstrate your Faith to those who are lost.

- Pray that you will consciously be aware of the Process of Faith in everything and every area of your life.

- Pray that you will walk through the Process of Faith every time you claim one of the promises of God.

- Pray that others will understand the Process of Faith.

# CHAPTER 6

# 36 Blessings of Faith

As we begin this chapter, please read this confession aloud: "*I can have everything the Bible says I can have, I can be everything the Bible says I can be, and I can do everything the Bible says I can do. Today I'm going to let the Word become life in my life.*"

As mentioned, the Bible offers a lot of promises. *For **all the promises** of God in him are yea, and in him Amen, unto the glory of God by us* (2 Corinthians 1:20). All the promises are ours, but we need to say amen to each individual one, as we have Faith to receive it. *And it shall come to pass, **if thou shalt hearken diligently** unto the voice of the LORD thy God, to observe and to do all his commandments which I command thee this day, that the LORD thy God will set thee on high above all nations of the earth: And **all these blessings shall come on thee**, and overtake thee if thou shalt hearken unto the voice of the LORD thy God* (Deuteronomy 28:1–2).

All these promises come by Faith, but you receive them by applying the Three Aspects of Faith we learned in chapter one. First, we must hear the promise (Word of Faith), we must keep God's law and know that the promise is a legal transaction from Heaven to us (Law of Faith), and then we must allow it to become life in our life (Spirit of Faith). And you will experience them to some degree in one of The Five Levels of Faith. You'll share them to a degree in Little Faith, or you may experience that same promise in Great Faith.

I have found 8,630 promises in the Word of God for you and me. That's 23 daily promises for a year with one hour to pray. I will share 36 of those in this chapter. As I said, that should keep you busy for more than a year.

These promises include every area of your life. They are not just for when we die, or when we all get to Heaven — that's one promise. Some are for us right now. The Apostle Paul prays that Man's whole spirit, soul, and body can be preserved blameless now (1 Thessalonians 5:23). Man is a spirit; he possesses a soul of mind, will, and emotions and lives in a house called a body. The blessings of God cover every part of our being: spirit, mind, emotions, will, physical, and monetary.

## Salvation

*For by grace are ye **saved through Faith**; and that not of yourselves: it is the gift of God* (Ephesians 2:8). This promise pertains to the spiritual realm and the soul realm. When our spirit man is saved or, as some refer to this, born again. *Being born again, not of corruptible seed, but of incorruptible, by the Word of God, which liveth and abideth forever* (1 Peter 1:23). When you believe in your heart and confess Jesus as Lord, you are saved by Faith in the incorruptible Word of God. Salvation is the Law of Faith; yes, that's a legal right. If you have Faith, the law says you will be saved.

Salvation also includes the salvation of your soul, mind, will, and emotions (see Hebrews 10:39). In your mental realm, many imaginations and thoughts need to be cast down. *Casting down imaginations, and every high thing that exalteth itself against the knowledge of God and **bringing into captivity every thought to the obedience of Christ*** (2 Corinthians 10:5). We continue casting down thoughts and imaginations until we have the mind of Christ. When we develop the mind of Christ, we will know Him by the Spirit and not just according to our flesh knowledge (see 2 Corinthians 5:16). Our emotions will then begin to line up with the mind of Christ, and we will have *peace that passes all understanding* (Philippians 4:7).

This salvation includes our will or purpose in life. Even Jesus had to deal with His will in the garden, saying, *Father, if thou be willing, remove this cup from me: nevertheless**, not my will, but thine, be done*** (Luke 22:42). I know giving up your will sounds a little scary, but trust me, the will and purpose of God for your life will exceed all you could ever hope for. *Now unto him that is able to do **exceedingly abundantly above all that we ask or think**, according to the power that worketh in us* (Ephesians 3:20).

The salvation of our mind, will, and emotions will be a Faith journey. Every day we will have thoughts and emotions that will challenge us, but through the power of Faith in the different levels of Faith, we can overcome and truly experience the blessing of salvation.

# Healing

*The same heard Paul speak: who steadfastly beholding him, and **perceiving that he had Faith to be healed*** (Acts 14:9). Healing for our bodies is one of the blessings and promises of Faith. Jesus paid for our healing by receiving thirty-nine stripes on his back. *Who his own self bare our sins in his own body on the tree, that we, being dead to sins, should live unto righteousness: **by whose stripes ye were healed*** (1 Peter 2:24). The blood of Jesus has established a legal contract for our healing; you can be healed because it is The Law of Faith. Preachers have told me that healing is not for today; it passed away with the disciples. All I can say to you is that I have seen blind eyes open, deaf ears unstopped, and disabled people walk in my forty years of ministry. I am approaching seventy years old and do not have any pain in my body. I'm on no medication, and I have walked in divine health for forty years, so it is a little too late to tell me that healing isn't around now. Healing is a blessing and promise by Faith, so if you don't believe and have Faith, you won't experience it today. Jesus paid the price with stripes on His back for you to have healing, so enjoy this blessing in your life today by Faith.

At the end of his ministry, the Apostle John shares his greatest desire for the people of God. *Beloved, **I wish above all things** that thou mayest **prosper and be in health**, even as thy soul prospereth* (3 John 2). Two of the greatest needs in people's lives today are their health and financial condition. Your Heavenly Father knows you have these needs and has given us the promise of healing and prosperity. I like to say it this way: I pray you have all the necessary finances to accomplish your ministry and a healthy enough body to do it in. Again, we receive these promises as we walk through the Three Aspects of Faith—The Word of Faith, The Law of Faith, and The Spirit of Faith. We will experience these promises in the Little Faith or Great Faith levels.

## Whole

*But Jesus turned him about, and when he saw her, he said, Daughter, be of good comfort; **thy_Faith hath made thee whole**. And the woman was **made whole from that hour*** (Matthew 9:22). *And Jesus said unto him, Go thy way; **thy Faith hath made thee whole**. And **immediately, he received his sight and** followed Jesus in the way* (Mark 10:52). Sometimes, when a person gets sick, they may have lingering symptoms or results of that sickness or disease. You might get healed of a rash, but your skin needs to return to newness. You might get rid of a disease, but you still have the effects; maybe you're still tired, worn out, or weak, and you need more time to recover. Healing is the start, but wholeness is the second and necessary step in your recovery. In the above verse, we saw that the woman began her recovery from that very hour. I'm not sure how long it took, but she was on the road to recovery. The man received his sight immediately. Either one works for me — how about you?

## Righteousness

*Even **the righteousness of God which is by the Faith** of Jesus Christ unto all and upon all them that believe: for there is no difference: For all have sinned, and come short of the glory of God* (Romans 3:22). We have to break the mindset that if we just do enough right things, we'll be in right standing with God. It doesn't matter how many things you do for your boss, spouse, or coworker, they will probably point out the one thing you did not do. The scripture is clear: God knows you have sinned and will sin and has provided the only way to be in right standing with Him, by Faith. God does not simply point out our sins but points out the faith that can take us out of that sin.

## Speak to Mountains

*And Jesus answering saith unto them,* **Have Faith in God***. For verily I say unto you, That whosoever shall* **say unto this mountain***, Be thou removed, and be thou cast into the sea; and shall not doubt in his heart, but shall believe that those things which he saith shall come to pass; he shall have whatsoever he saith. Therefore, I say unto you, What things soever ye desire, when ye pray, believe that ye receive them, and ye shall have them* (Mark 11:22–24). What's the mountain standing in your way, the big thing stopping you from moving forward? Is it the fear of failure, sickness, tiredness, or the lack of money? If you don't speak to that cough, if you don't speak to that pain, if you don't speak to that mountain — if you don't speak to it, it's not going anywhere. Whatever that mountain is — they come in all shapes and sizes — it stops you from getting any further in your mission.

The other day, I had facial swelling and fluid pooling in my right cheek. My wife asked me what I was doing about it. I realized I was doing nothing about it and just believing God that I was healed. Yes, I slipped back into casual Faith, which was No Faith. I had my wife lay her hand on my cheek, and

I began to speak to my sinus and command the blockage to dissolve and be removed. Immediately I felt a tingling in my nose, and it was all gone within an hour. Nothing would have changed until I spoke to it. I had no evidence of my Faith until I talked to it. Speak to your mountain today.

## Purified Hearts

*And put no difference between us and them, **purifying their hearts by Faith*** (Acts 15:9). How do you get a pure heart? Only by Faith are you going to cleanse your attitude; the harder you try to wash your attitude with yourself, the more attitude you get. *That the **trial of your Faith**, being much more precious than of gold that perisheth, though it be **tried with fire**, might be found unto praise and honor and glory at the appearing of Jesus Christ* (1 Peter 1:7). Your Faith is going to be tried, but after the fire, your Faith will shine like gold. Your "attitude" about Faith will change and move from "I have to believe God" to "It is a joy to believe God." *Looking unto Jesus, the **author and finisher of our Faith**, who for the joy that was set before him endured the cross, despising the shame, and is set down at the right hand of the throne of God* (Hebrews 12:2). There is an old song that goes like this: He who has begun a good work in you will be faithful to complete it. Another song goes like this: Even when I can't see you working, you are still working in me.

## Churches Established

*And so were **the churches established in the Faith** and increased in number daily* (Acts 16:5). How are many churches established today? Secular marketing, church splits, goat gatherings, and I better stop there before I get meddling. Churches need to be established and made solid by Faith, which is the evidence of God's Word saving, healing, and transforming lives. When people see the real power of God, they will flock to the church, and the numbers will increase daily.

# Sanctification

*To open their eyes, and to turn them from darkness to light, and from the power of Satan unto God, that they may receive forgiveness of sins, and inheritance among them which are **sanctified by Faith** that is in me* (Acts 26:18). Sanctification is a lost word in churches today. Many will say, "God loves me just the way I am." I agree, but God loves you enough not to leave you the way you are but to open your eyes to the darkness or the ignorance that keeps you from seeing God's promises for your life. God loves you enough to break the power of Satan off your life, forgive you, and give you an inheritance as a child of God. Everyone must take the garbage out weekly, clean the refrigerator, and wash the dirty laundry. So too must you throw out your flaws and wash away your sins. God wants to clean out the old so He can bring in the new.

# Testimony

*First, I thank my God through Jesus Christ for you all, that **your Faith is spoken of throughout the whole world*** (Romans 1:8). I was on the phone with a computer tech, and at the end of it, he said, "I just want to thank you for your patience today. I don't believe I've ever had a customer with more patience than you have." I was a testimony to him, but he did not know he was talking about my Faith on trial. I fought the good fight of Faith because things were not looking good, and when things are not looking good, you tend to have a test of patience. What impressed him was why I did not get impatient. Apparently, he deals with people who have no patience every day. They want him to fix their problems and fix them now. If your testimony brings more attention to you, it's not a testimony according to God. He was so impressed with me but was impressed with my patience, which came from the trying of my Faith and comes from God. I said this is a Godly principle that I've let become "life in my life." I gave the glory back to God. Many people talk about their Faith, but can others see it in action in the intense moments?

## Won't Fail

*But I have prayed for thee, that **thy Faith fail not**: and when thou art converted, strengthen thy brethren* (Luke 22:32). When do we need this promise? As soon as I hit the problem, I've reached failure. I already have the pain, I already have the ache, and I've already failed, but my Faith isn't going to fail; my Faith is going to change the failure. When you have a problem, this is the moment to apply this promise.

## Strong

*And his name **through Faith in his name hath made this man strong**, whom ye see and know: yea, the Faith which is by him hath given him this perfect soundness in the presence of you all* (Acts 3:16). They come to the apostles and say, "You guys are superheroes; you are the healers." The apostles reply, "Don't look at us. It's not by some great thing we've done. Faith in the name of Jesus made this man strong" (Acts 3:1–12). We need to get to the place where we don't take the credit; it is by Faith. Real strength comes from Faith.

## Miracles

*He therefore that ministereth to you the Spirit, and **worketh miracles** among you, doeth he it by the works of the law, or **by the hearing of Faith**?* (Galatians 3:5). *How* do miracles happen? By Faith. Are miracles for today? Well, Faith is for today, and that is how miracles happen.

## Children of Abraham

*Know ye therefore that **they which are of Faith**, the same are the **children of Abraham*** (Galatians 3:7). The blessings promised to Abraham become ours; we inherit all the promises given to Abraham, Isaac, and Jacob. We have many of these promises through inheritance because, by Faith, we are the children of Abraham.

### Blessed—In a Position to Receive from God

*So, then **they which be of Faith are blessed** with faithful Abraham* (Galatians 3:9). I like to explain the word blessed as simply being "in a position" to receive from God. Faith puts us in that position to receive all the promises, but we must know what they are to have Faith for them.

### Children of God

*For ye are all **the children of God by Faith** in Christ Jesus* (Galatians 3:26). By Faith in Jesus, we are brought into the family of God.

### Living by Faith

*But that no man is justified by the law in the sight of God, it is evident: for,* ***The just shall live by Faith*** (Galatians 3:11). I remind you again of the message of this book: "Let the Word become life in your life!"

### Receive the Spirit

*This only would I learn of you,* ***Received ye the Spirit*** *by the works of the law, or* ***by the hearing of Faith?*** *Are ye so foolish? Having begun in the Spirit, are ye now made perfect by the flesh?* (Galatians 3:2–3). We start this journey in Faith and receive blessings, don't shift back to the flesh efforts to obtain anything.

*That the blessing of Abraham might come on the Gentiles through Jesus Christ; that we might* ***receive the promise of the Spirit through Faith*** (Galatians 3:14). God desires you to have His Spirit in you. *Even the Spirit of truth; whom the world cannot receive, because it seeth him not, neither knoweth him: but ye know him; for he dwelleth with you and shall be in you* (John 14:17).

# Justified

*Therefore, being* ***justified by Faith****, we have peace with God through our Lord Jesus Christ:* (Romans 5:1). God is the judge, and He can legally declare us justified when we put our Faith in Him.

*Wherefore the law was our schoolmaster to bring us unto Christ, that we might be* ***justified by Faith*** (Galatians 3:24). God uses His Torah, His Law as a schoolteacher to bring us to

Faith in His wisdom, love, sacrifice, and correction to justify us for our purpose in life.

## Strong and Not Stagger

*And being not weak in Faith, he considered not his own body now dead, when he was about a hundred years old, neither yet the deadness of Sarah's womb: He **staggered not at the promise of God** through unbelief; but was **strong in Faith**, giving glory to God; And being fully persuaded that, what he had promised, he was able also to perform. And therefore, it was imputed to him for righteousness* (Romans 4:19–22). You may be staggering at some of God's promises, thinking they are too good to be true. Can God really do this with me? Can that really happen to me? Maybe I'm too old or too young? The answer is yes; nothing is impossible with God. If He promised it, He will bring it to pass in your life; just stay in Faith.

## Access

*Therefore, being justified by Faith, we have peace with God through our Lord Jesus Christ: By whom also **we have access by Faith** into this grace wherein we stand and rejoice in the hope of the glory of God* (Romans 5:1–2).

*In whom we have **boldness and access with confidence by the Faith** of him* (Ephesians 3:12). By now, you should realize all of this is by Faith and not your good works or canceled by your failures. We come boldly to His throne with the Three Aspects of Faith and receive according to our level of Faith.

## Wiser than the Wisdom of Men

*That your Faith should not stand in the **wisdom of men, but in the power of God*** (1 Corinthians 2:5). Our nature is to try to figure Faith out. I want to save you some wasted time; you can't and never will figure it out using the wisdom of men. Faith is simply *trusting* the wisdom of God; He knows what He is doing. He knows the future and is able, by His power, to bring it to pass.

## Walk by Faith

*For we **walk by Faith**, not by sight* (2 Corinthians 5:7). This does not mean closing your eyes and walking mindlessly. We close our eyes to the natural circumstances and see the possibility of God's Word. We know what God wants to do in our life and walk by Faith in each promise.

## Indwelling

***That Christ may dwell in your hearts by Faith**; that ye, being rooted and grounded in love* (Ephesians 3:17). I am sure you've heard people say that they asked Jesus to come into their heart. You may have even said this yourself. Bear with me for a moment as I try to explain this. Getting a five-foot, nine-inch Jewish man named Jesus to move into your body will be difficult. The verse says that "Christ" may dwell in your heart. The word Christ in the Greek, *Christos,* means *anointing, to be anointed*. Paul says the anointing that Jesus walked in may dwell in you. Jesus said the works that he did, you will also do, and He knew you would never be able to do them without the anointing or indwelling of His Spirit. When you face a problem bigger than yourself, have Faith in the anointing that dwells within you.

## Shield of Faith

*Above all, taking **the shield of Faith**, wherewith ye shall be able to quench all the fiery darts of the wicked* (Ephesians 6:16). Sometimes, we do not need to be on the offensive. Sometimes in the heat of the battle, the wise thing may be to just step behind your shield of Faith until all the fiery darts, thoughts, and words go by.

## Nourished and Fed

*If thou put the brethren in remembrance of these things, thou shalt be a good minister of Jesus Christ, **nourished up in the words of Faith** and of **good doctrine**, whereunto thou hast attained* (1 Timothy 4:6). Pastors and ministers often get so busy doing the ministry and feeding others the Word that they don't take time to feed themselves. Soon they will have old manna, old sermons that are not a fresh Word from God today. God said to pray to *give us this day our daily bread* (Matthew 6:11). God has a fresh Word for you today; take time to be nourished and then give out again.

## Creative Words

*That **the communication of thy Faith** may become effectual by the acknowledging of every good thing which is in you in Christ Jesus* (Philemon 1:6). We are born creators; God is the creator, and we are his children created in his image and likeness. Please wait a minute. Are you saying we are creators?

Now that is going too far. Consider it for a moment; we can create a mess, a war with our words, and strife. How about communicating God's Word to create peace, joy, healing, and every good thing that is in you in Christ Jesus? You will say something today; use your words for God's purpose.

## Inherit Promises

*That ye be not slothful, but followers of them who **through Faith and patience inherit the promises*** (Hebrews 6:12). The wisdom Paul gives us in this scripture tells us we are going to follow somebody, so why not follow someone who, through Faith and patience, has inherited the promises of God with evidence and proof that the promises work in their life? When we do so, we can be confident that we will also inherit the promises through faith and patience. Refrain from following those who are all talk and no show.

## Substance and Evidence

*Now **Faith is the substance** of things hoped for, **the evidence** of things not seen*** (Hebrews 11:1). Don't just stop at hope; keep applying your Faith until you have the substance. I have a good marriage. I am not just saying it or hoping for it. I have a good marriage. I have a healthy body, and when at our church, they play a song that says, "I will run, and I will dance," I don't just stand there and sing it. I take off and run around the sanctuary and dance before the Lord. I joke with the congregation that I'm the oldest person in the sanctuary, so there is no excuse for them. Many of them run with me now — and what a joy that is that fills the sanctuary. Having substance to your Faith is a promise; claim it today.

## Please God

*But **without Faith, it is impossible to please him**: for he that cometh to God must believe that he is, and that he is a rewarder of them that diligently seek him* (Hebrews 11:6). God finds pleasure when we trust Him and act on His Word. God was pleased when Peter exited the boat to walk on water. So what? He only took three steps and then began to sink. God was still delighted to see him try but had no pleasure in the other eleven hiding in the boat out of fear. Please know that whatever level of Faith you are at, or even if you fail, God finds pleasure every time you try.

## Patience

*Knowing this, that the **trying of your Faith worketh patience*** (James 1:3). I heard a preacher say don't ask God for patience because He will give you an opportunity to develop it immediately. The Greek word for patience is *hupomone—cheerful, hopeful of endurance and constancy, continuance, enduring, and patient.* When we have a trial of Faith, we need to approach the test with a cheerful and hopeful mindset. If we understand that the trial simply helps us to become more consistent in our Faith, we will look at the test as a helper instead of an enemy. Patience does not mean putting up with it but developing consistent joy when faced with trials. Consistency will aid us in developing a lifestyle of Faith. When your test of Faith comes, be glad that God is working a fun and positive lifestyle of Faith in you.

# Salvation of Your Soul

*Receiving* **the end of your Faith***, even* **the salvation of your souls** (1 Peter 1:9). Faith is a journey throughout our lives. I have said many times that we are saved, being saved, and will be saved. We start with our spirit being saved, then we are being saved, which involves our soul, mind, will, and emotions, and that takes a little time. This scripture brings us hope for peace in our souls, even during war, famines, and economic disasters. When everything around us is in turmoil, we can have the Kingdom of God within us. *The Kingdom of God is righteousness, peace, and joy in the Holy Ghost* (Romans 14:17). Don't be disappointed that your Faith has not changed everything and everyone around; you have received the end of your Faith, the salvation of your soul.

# Victory That Overcomes the World

*For whatsoever is born of God overcometh the world: and* **this is the victory that overcometh the world, even our Faith** (1 John 5:4). What world must we overcome? World in the Greek is *kosmon—selfishness, lies, deception, and decorations to impress.* As you can see by the definitions, the world will take your time and life away from the spiritual realm of the Kingdom of God and cause you to focus on your own selfish desires. The world will offer everything glamorous and inviting to man's fleshly desires. The world will make empty promises that eventually disappoint. We overcome all this with the truth of God's promises that are not empty but exceedingly abundantly above all we could ask and think. As we experience God's promises, the world will slowly become dim, less exciting, and dull.

## Powerful Prayer Life

*But let him **ask in Faith**, nothing wavering. For he that wavereth is like a wave of the sea driven with the wind and tossed* (James 1:6). As we receive this blessing, our prayer life changes dramatically. We no longer come to God as a beggar, hoping He will do something, but we ask in Faith, knowing He will honor His Word.

*And **the prayer of Faith shall save the sick**, and the Lord shall raise him up; and if he has committed sins, they shall be forgiven him* (James 5:15). In the level of Great Faith, our prayer of Faith will have the power to bring healing to the sick, raise one from a death grip, and forgive sins to those who have lost hope.

*But ye, beloved, **building up yourselves on your most holy Faith, praying in the Holy Ghost*** (Jude 1:20). The Holy Spirit within you knows exactly what to pray when we, in our natural understanding, do not. How often do you try to build yourself up, encourage yourself, and talk to yourself? All that is good, but how much more practical building of your faith can be done if you take the time to pray in the Spirit?

## Unity

*Till we all come in the **unity of the Faith**, and of the knowledge of the Son of God, unto a perfect man, unto the measure of the stature of the fullness of Christ* (Ephesians 4:13). I saved this one for last. As you can see, it is hard to believe unity is possible. It is hard to find unity in marriages today. It's hard to find it in families today. It's hard to find it among bosses and employees today. Sadly, it is even hard to find it in churches today. Many try to bring conformity with compromise, bribes, and passiveness but never produce true unity, only a dumbing down of beliefs. Nonetheless, it is a promise of God, and it only takes Faith to bring it into our lives. But, it will take more than a bit of Faith, might even take more than Great Faith; we might have to get level five of Full of Faith. I ask that you step in and agree with me that as we, through Faith, make a place for God to reveal His Word and pour out His anointing, change will begin. I pray for marriages, families, businesses, and churches to come into the unity of Faith and grow in Faith until their Faith is full. Amen.

## Questions:

- Have you considered how many blessings Faith brings to you?
- Have you tried to be blessed without Faith?
- Why are people not blessed?
- What blessings by Faith stand out to you?
- How do you see that this year can be a year of blessing?
- How does Faith bring blessings?
- What do you need to change for blessings to come into your life?
- Can you truly be blessed without hearing The Word of Faith?

## Prayer Focus:

- Pray that you will see and recognize that God desires you to be blessed.
- Pray that the Holy Spirit will reveal the blessings you need to receive now.
- Pray that you will apply the Three Aspects of Faith to receive them.
- Pray that you will experience them to a degree according to your level of Faith.
- Pray that you remember the blessings come by Faith and not by works.
- Pray and make your confessions for the blessings according to the Word.
- Pray that you will make living the promised blessing by Faith a daily priority.
- Pray that this year will be a year of blessings.
- Pray that you will hear and receive the "36 Blessings of Faith" throughout this year.
- Pray that the Holy Spirit will give you the power to walk and operate in Faith, resisting the doubts of the flesh.
- Pray that your life will be pleasing to the Lord as you walk in the blessings of Faith.
- Pray that your life will show substance and evidence of the blessing.

# CHAPTER 7
# Keep the Faith

As we begin this chapter, please read this confession aloud: *"I can have everything the Bible says I can have, I can be everything the Bible says I can be, and I can do everything the Bible says I can do. Today I'm going to let the Word become life in my life."*

Once you've gone through the Process of Faith and you're trying to increase in the Levels of Faith and trying to remember the Three Aspects of Faith and how to apply them, a test will come. Learning is fun, but you will probably remember from school that there is an occasional pop quiz and the dreaded test after the lesson. Oh no! Do I know what I believe, and can I apply the answers during the test? Relax, and take a deep breath; you'll be surprised about how you'll be able to breeze through the test and ace it.

## Will He Find Faith?

*When the Son of man cometh,* **shall he find Faith on the earth?** (Luke 18:8). When Jesus returns, He will look for Faith. Aren't you glad you're increasing your Faith? Apparently, when He returns, Faith may be hard to find. He's not looking for people who call themselves Christians and not looking for people that are religious and try to act like Christians. What's Jesus looking for: true Faith, the kind you're learning about, the type of Faith with evidence and substance that has stood the test of time.

## Continue in the Faith

*Confirming the souls of the disciples, and exhorting them to **continue in the Faith**, and that **we must through much tribulation enter into the kingdom of God*** (Acts 14:22). The Apostle Paul is confirming (Confirming in the *Greek —episterizo—reestablish, strengthen)* the disciples after undergoing some tough tests. He encouraged the disciples to continue, persevere, and stay strong in their souls, minds, will, and emotions. If you get through the tests, tribulations, and trials, you will find yourself in God's kingdom, where there is righteousness, peace, and joy in the Holy Ghost (see Romans 14:17). In the last forty years of my ministry, I have found that tribulations are not just a one-time event. I have found that, every year, there is a final exam you must pass to graduate for the following year. I have continued in Faith all these years, and so can you.

## Keep the Commandments by Faith

*Here is the **patience of the saints**: here are they that **keep the commandments of God, and the Faith of Jesus*** (Revelation 14:12). The Apostle John knows what he's talking about because he's been through every test imaginable and tells us patience is the key to keeping the commandments of God. Jesus summed up the ten commandments by saying love God and love others (Matthew 22:37–38). Loving God is easy, but loving others will require patience with them and maybe a lot of Faith.

## Contend for the Faith

*Beloved, when I gave all diligence to write unto you of the common salvation, it was needful for me to write unto you and exhort you that **ye should earnestly contend for the Faith** which was once delivered unto the saints* (Jude 1:3). One of the reasons I was diligent about writing this book was to encourage people to contend for the Faith that was delivered by the Apostles. Faith has become a watered-down, sloppy agape, greasy Grace, and powerless gospel preached today. Join me today to contend for the Faith that brings results into your life and others during the tests, not just a sweet by-and-by gospel for Sundays. Remember, the Devil does not want Jesus to find true Faith when He returns.

## Resist in the Faith

*Be sober, be vigilant; because your adversary, the Devil, as a roaring lion, walketh about, seeking whom he may devour: Whom **resist steadfast in the Faith**, knowing that the same afflictions are accomplished in your brethren that are in the world* (1 Peter 5:8). If Jesus is looking for Faith when he returns, what do you think the Devil is looking for? No Faith, weak Faith, somebody that's about ready to give up their Faith, and someone that will not take a stand and contend for the Faith. When the enemy comes with his sickness, disease, sin, poverty, and battles to get you to give up your Faith, resist him steadfastly in the Faith. Take the Devil to the courts of Heaven and The Law of Faith, and win your case. Move into compassion for others going through these same afflictions and use your Great Faith to make a difference in their life.

## Holding Faith

***Holding Faith,*** *and a good conscience, which some having put away concerning Faith, have made shipwreck* (1 Timothy 1:19). Your conscience is a good thermometer to show the level of Faith you're at. Some have put away *(Greek apotheomai—push off, reject, surrender, cease)* their Faith and have gone shipwreck. Listen to your conscience; it will tell you if you're getting off course. How many times has that still, small voice warned you not to do something, but you did it anyway? Keep both hands on the wheel of Faith, hold tight, and don't let go until you've reached your destination. I've heard many say, "Well, God is my pilot, and I'm just the passenger." This phrase sounds so good and humble, but God created you with a will, and you can steer your life wherever you want. Of course, if you are living in Faith, you will steer where God, your GPS, guides you. Faith is God's way of teaching you to drive in this life, but you're responsible for following the directions.

## Fight the Good Fight of Faith

***Fight the good fight of Faith****, lay hold on eternal life, whereunto thou art also called, and hast professed a good profession before many witnesses* (1 Timothy 6:12). First, you must know it's a good fight, not a bad one! You will need to change the mindset of "Oh, no! I have to fight for my Faith." If you don't use Faith, it's a nasty fight; you'll never win the battle without Faith. Next, you need to lay hold on eternal life *(eternal in the Greek—aionios—past, present, future, perpetual)*. This fight will be ongoing and endless, but the good news is that in each fight of Faith, we will be a great witness to others as they see us win our battles. I'm transparent with my ministers and let them know when I'm going through a fight of Faith. They all know when I tell them that I'll have a testimony soon because they know I'm going "through" and not stopping until I win. I assure you right now that you can get through your battle because you're fighting the good fight of Faith.

## Keep the Faith

*I have fought a good fight, I have finished my course, **I have kept the Faith*** (2 Timothy 4:7). I can believe Paul when he says this because I have found that his Faith was reliable. He shook off snakes, dealt with a shipwreck, fasted, pressed through the persecution of people talking about him, and being thrown in prison. Yet, through it all, he continued in Faith. He didn't quit the ministry and finished his course. Over the years, I've found a valuable key in this fight: to not focus on the battle but to fight to Keep the Faith. When you realize the enemy's purpose is to steal your Faith, you will focus on the real issue, which is your Faith. As soon as you decide to Keep the Faith, you will find that you have already won the battle.

## The Trying of Your Faith

*Knowing this, that **the trying of your Faith** worketh patience* (James 1:3). "Knowing this" is crucial. Once you realize the trying of your Faith is to work patience in your life, you go into this process with joy and anticipation of the results that God is working on in your life. God is building a consistent lifestyle of Faith in your life. Every time a test comes, your lifestyle of Faith increases, and you begin to act in Faith in each battle. Each victory prepares you for the next fight; your response is the same, even if the fight is more challenging.

I know this may sound silly, but I've used my Faith in some ridiculous little things I've had to deal with on a daily basis. For example, the ice maker in the refrigerator was making noise, meaning I would have to replace the motor, which would cost me money. Yes, you guessed it. I laid my hands on the refrigerator. The noise stopped, and it's still working today. I would lay hands on my cows for healing, and the veterinarian who came monthly for a herd checkup would tell me I had the healthiest herd in my region. You may laugh, but I thought I would try this out on my cows before trying it on people. My Faith increased, and now I've laid my hands on thousands of people who have received healing. I tell people to practice their Faith with the ache, pain, and flu before they try tackling cancer. If you don't try, you can be sure nothing will happen. You'll be surprised how God finds joy in your little acts of Faith.

## The Author and Finisher of Our Faith

*Looking unto Jesus, the **author and finisher of our Faith**, who for the joy that was set before him endured the cross, despising the shame, and is set down at the right hand of the throne of God* (Hebrews 12:2). Who better to help you finish your Faith than the one who died and rose again, the one that took thirty-nine stripes on his back for your healing, the one who had a spear in his side, the one who had nails in his hands and feet? Jesus knew how to get through it all and is seated with God the Father in Heavenly places. He knows how to finish and is now our author and finisher of our Faith. What Jesus has started in you, He will be faithful to complete it. When you catch a glimpse of the joy of your finished Faith, you too will be able to get through carrying your cross and ignoring the shame and sit with Him in Heavenly places.

## Some Shall Depart from the Faith

*Now the Spirit speaketh expressly, that in the latter times, some shall **depart from the Faith**, giving heed to seducing spirits, and doctrines of Devils* (1 Timothy 4:1). The Holy Spirit is speaking that there will be an onslaught of lying, seducing spirits, and wrong doctrine that will cause many to give up on their Faith. I encourage you to be the one that holds on, fights, and keeps the Faith.

## Continue in the Faith

*If ye **continue in the Faith** grounded and settled, and be not moved away from the hope of the gospel, which ye have heard, and which was preached to every creature which is under Heaven; whereof I Paul am made a minister* (Colossians 1:23). Settle it in your heart today, stay grounded, and refuse to move away from the hope of all that God has for you to enjoy. You have heard enough of the Word of God and experienced enough evidence to stop in your journey of Faith now. I love this particular commercial on TV about an insurance company; their phrase is, "I know a thing or two because I've seen a thing or two." Continue in the Faith by walking through the Process of Faith, the Aspects of Faith, and growing in your level of Faith; soon, you will be known as a minister of God to others because you know a thing or two and have seen a thing or two.

## Where Is Your Faith?

*And he said unto them, **where is your Faith?** And they being afraid, wondered, saying one to another, What manner of man is this! for He commandeth even the winds and water, and they obey him* (Luke 8:25). Have you ever felt this way?

Where is my Faith? Did I leave it at church? I thought I had Faith just a minute ago. I joke sometimes and say Faith is like a woman's purse. I believe they have everything in there — they have tape, scissors, pens, money, knives, I even think they have pipe wrenches, and oh yes, they have makeup. If you need something, it's in a woman's purse, but it's hard to find the item you need as it can get lost in there. Like Faith, though you have it in your heart and mind, you may have to look for it for a moment, but be encouraged, you have it in there. You don't have to be in a hurry with your Faith. Take your time to find it, pull it out, and use it.

## Your Faith Fail Not

*But I have prayed for thee, that* **thy Faith fail not**: *and when thou art converted, strengthen thy brethren* (Luke 22:32). Jesus is not saying His miraculous prayer will cause Faith to work in your life from now on. He is not praying that you won't fail. Jesus is praying that **your** Faith will not fail. I can pray that your Faith will not fail, but I can't live your Faith for you. But, don't worry. Your Faith, based on your Faith level, will not fail. Little Faith will work in some areas, and Great Faith will work in more significant areas.

## Faith Spoken Of

*First, I thank my God through Jesus Christ for you all, that* **your Faith is spoken of** *throughout the whole world* (Romans 1:8). Rather than trying to impress people with all you do for God, let your Faith speak. While you're being tested, people will watch you as you apply and walk in Faith, bringing substance and evidence into their midst, and people will see it and talk about your Faith.

## Remember It Was Faith, Not You

*All the commandments which I command thee this day shall ye observe to do, that ye may live, and multiply, and **go in and possess the land** which the LORD sware unto your fathers. And thou shalt **remember** all the way which the LORD thy God <u>led</u> thee these forty years in the wilderness, to **humble** thee, and to **prove** thee, to know what was in thine heart, whether thou wouldest keep his commandments, or no. And **he humbled thee**, and suffered thee to hunger, and **fed thee with manna**, which thou knewest not, neither did thy fathers know; **that he might make thee know that man doth not live by bread only, but by every word that proceedeth out of the mouth of the LORD doth man live*** (Deuteronomy 8:1–3). God told the children of Israel that if they kept His commandments *(His wisdom, His instructions, His Word)*, they would live, multiply, and possess the land. In other words, if they believe, obey His Word, and walk in Faith, they will have His blessings in their life. The main word we need to see here is *remember*. It is easy to begin thinking we accomplished all these great things and take the credit. God reminds you that it was He who led you, humbled you, fed you, provided for you, proved you, and brought you to the understanding that it was The Word of Faith that came from your mouth that caused you to live and enjoy these blessings.

*Thy raiment waxed not old upon thee, neither did thy foot swell, these forty years. Thou shalt also consider in thine heart, that, as a man chasteneth his son, so the LORD thy God chasteneth thee. Therefore **thou shalt keep the commandments of the LORD thy God, to walk in his ways**, and to fear him. For **the LORD thy God bringeth thee into a good land**, a land of brooks of water, of fountains and depths that spring* *out of valleys and hills;* ***A land of wheat****, and* ***barley****, and* ***vines****, and* ***fig trees****, and* ***pomegranates****; a land* ***of oil olive****, and* ***honey****; A land wherein thou shalt eat* ***bread without scarceness****, thou shalt* ***not lack anything*** *in it; a land whose stones are* ***iron****, and out of whose hills thou mayest dig* ***brass****.* ***When thou hast eaten and art full, then thou shalt bless the LORD thy God for the good land which he hath given thee*** (Deuteronomy 8:4–10). God again reminds you that He will continue to correct and instruct even after He brings you into the excellent land of provision where you lack nothing.

*Beware that thou forget not the LORD thy God, in not keeping his commandments, and his judgments, and his statutes, which I command thee this day: Lest when thou hast eaten and art full, and hast built goodly houses, and dwelt therein; And when thy herds and thy flocks multiply, and thy silver and thy gold is multiplied, and all that thou hast is multiplied; Then thine heart be lifted up, and thou forget the LORD thy God, which brought thee forth out of the land of Egypt, from the house of bondage; Who led thee through that great and terrible wilderness, wherein were fiery serpents, and scorpions, and drought, where there was no water; who brought thee forth water out of the rock of flint;* ***Who fed thee in the wilderness with manna****, which thy fathers knew not, that he might humble thee, and that he might prove thee, to do thee good at thy latter end;* ***And thou say in thine heart, My power and the might of mine hand hath gotten me this wealth****. But* ***thou shalt remember the LORD thy God: for it is he that giveth thee power to get wealth, that he may establish his covenant*** *which he sware unto thy fathers, as it is this day. And it shall be, if thou do at all forget the LORD thy God, and walk after other gods, and serve them, and worship* *them, I testify against you this day that ye shall surely perish. As the nations which the LORD destroyeth before your face, so shall ye perish, because ye would not be obedient unto the voice of the LORD your God* (Deuteronomy 8:11–20). Here comes a strong warning: If we forget the Lord and His Word, stop keeping the instructions, start being consumed with our blessings, and fall into pride, it will be our downfall. We must *remember* that it has been God and Faith in His Word that have brought this wealth into our lives for the purpose of establishing His covenant on Earth. All these blessings in our life should be a witness to the nations that would cause them to want to serve God also encourages you to Keep the Faith so Jesus can find Faith in you when He returns. Continue in the Faith by keeping His commandments by Faith, and contend for the Faith when the battle comes. Resist in the Faith, hold on to your Faith, and fight the good fight of Faith so others will speak of your Faith.

As always, "Let the Word become life in your life."

## Questions:

- Why did the Apostle Paul say, "Keep the Faith"?
- What does it mean to "Keep the Faith"?
- What is the opposite of Keeping the Faith?
- What prevents you from Keeping the Faith?
- What does it mean to fight the good fight of Faith?
- Can anyone else Keep the Faith for you, or do you have to Keep the Faith for yourself?
- Why did Jesus say, "Will I find Faith on the Earth when I return"?

- How important is Keeping the Faith?
- Name one way you are going to Keep the Faith.

## Prayer Focus:

- Pray that the Holy Spirit will reveal the pressure and temptation to depart from the Faith.
- Pray that you will continue in the Faith.
- Pray that the Holy Spirit will reveal the areas where you're challenged in your walk of Faith.
- Pray and repent for departing from the Faith.
- Pray and study how you can fight the good fight of Faith.
- Pray for courage and discipline to continue and contend for the Faith.
- Pray that you will hold fast a good conscience of Faith.
- Pray that you will hold fast to your confession of Faith and not waver or become disobedient with your words.
- Pray that your actions will demonstrate your Faith.
- Pray that you will consciously be aware of the good fight of Faith and your real enemy of Faith.
- Pray that you will live by Faith each and every time you claim one of the promises of God.
- Pray that others will understand the good fight of Faith.

# CHAPTER 8

# The Holy Spirit Works in The Five Levels of Faith

As we begin this chapter, please read this confession aloud: *"I can have everything the Bible says I can have, I can be everything the Bible says I can be, and I can do everything the Bible says I can do. Today I'm going to let the Word become life in my life."*

You are not alone in your journey of Faith. The Holy Spirit, who is our helper, is with you every step of the way in each level of our Faith.

## The Five Levels of Faith and the Work of the Holy Spirit

- **The Measure of Faith** — *Conviction*
- **No Faith** — *Judgment*
- **Little Faith** — *Baptism*
- **Great Faith** — *Receive*
- **Full of Faith** — *Filled*

## How the Holy Spirit Works in the First Level of Faith — Conviction

*And when he comes,* **he will convict the world of its sin, and of God's righteousness, and of the coming judgment** (John 16:8). The Holy Spirit begins his work in the First Level of Faith—The Measure of Faith. His first work is to convict or show people their sin of missing the mark of all God has for them. Then He shows them they can be in right standing with God and receive His blessings and warns them of the coming judgment where they must account for what they've done with their lives.

**Let no corrupt communication proceed out of your mouth,** *but that which is good to the use of edifying, that it may minister Grace unto the hearers.* **And grieve not the Holy Spirit of God**, *whereby ye are sealed unto the day of redemption* (Ephesians 4:29–30). Corrupt communication is worthless, empty, hollow, and shallow talk that grieves the Holy Spirit because He can't do anything with those words, which are not Faith words.

## How the Holy Spirit Works in the Second Level of Faith — Judgment

**And this is the judgment**: *the light has come into the world, and* **people loved the darkness rather than the light** *because their works were evil. For everyone who does wicked things hates the light and does not come to the light, lest his works should be exposed. But whoever does what is true comes to the light, so that it may be clearly seen that his works have been carried out in God"* (John 3:19). The Holy Spirit is grieved and allows you to enter the second Level of Faith—No Faith. He waits patiently and resumes the work of convicting sin until you come back into Faith. He knows that, eventually, you will see the light again, repent, and confess your sin.

I hear religious people say, "Don't judge me!" but this scripture says that judgment has already come to you because of your choice and action. The Apostle John explains that the Holy Spirit has brought light and conviction to you; however, because you love darkness and would rather stay in the shadows, the judgment is that you turned away from the Holy Spirit's working. Apostle John continues and says that whoever chooses to come to light will allow the work of the Holy Spirit to take them to the next level of Faith.

I hear these phrases, "You don't know what you don't know," and "If you're deceived, you don't know it," and they're true. I've even said them when ministering to people. Let me ask you a question: After you've heard the Word and the Holy Spirit has brought conviction to you, how can you still say you don't know? Are you saying blindness and deception are more powerful than the Word and the Spirit? Sometimes I wonder if those are just convenient religious excuses to stay where you are and do what you want to do. I also know you're not living or doing the Word of God because it has not manifested in your life. I have said to people who've uttered these phrases that I believe they believe what they're saying. I don't mean it as a condescending statement but simply mean there's nothing I can do to change their belief. What can *I* do if the Word and the Spirit won't change it?

Do you want me to leave you where you're at? As a man of God, I can't help but keep preaching the Word of God to you until you let the Word become life in your life, so you can experience all that God has for you.

Some people say, "Well, just love me." What does that mean? Ignore your sin? Ignore your purpose in life, your call, your eternity, and your destiny. Do you want me to ignore those, too? Well, that kind of love means I don't care about you. Know that if I really love you, I want to tell you the Word. I want to tell you your fault. I will tell you where you're missing it and falling short of God's best for you. This is the vocabulary of level two, and yes, you're either going to say, "Yes, Lord, thank you for convicting me and for showing me" and move on, or you're going to grieve the Holy Spirit and move back to the level of No Faith. The intelligent thing to do is confess your sin and move to the next level.

We find, throughout scripture, how the Spirit of God uses the Men of God to bring judgment. Moses sat from morning to night, judging the people. The Prophets always brought a word of correction to the people of God. God's Spirit used the Apostle Paul to point out people's faults. The Spirit of God was moving through Apostle John to point out people's faults and sins and where they're missing them. Jesus brought judgment and correction to the Pharisees and even called them snakes, vipers, and hypocrites. Wow! I've asked my congregation, "Do you want me as your bishop to ignore your faults, never point out where you're missing it, and help you get back on track? What kind of bishop or pastor would that be?"

Judgment without redemption in mind is wrong. Redemption is the goal, and judgment is the process to help people get there. Judging people without a solution for their fault is nothing more than pride. But, when applied correctly, judgment is a biblical principle that will help people move to another level of Faith. I often use an example of a dirty diaper — someone needs to judge and change it and not ignore it in the name of love.

## How the Holy Spirit Works in the Third Level of Faith—Baptism

*Marvel not that I said unto thee,* ***Ye must be born again*** (John 3:7). The born-again experience is a supernatural work of the Holy Spirit of salvation in your life, securing that you will go to Heaven when you die. You cannot be born again by your own works; your part in this is to believe and receive this gift of Grace.

*Jesus answered and said unto him, Verily, verily, I say unto thee,* ***Except a man be born again, he cannot see the kingdom of God*** (John 3:3). Salvation, which is the first and most crucial step, is what you are or have been focusing on and thinking about. Now, the Holy Spirit works to help you see the Kingdom of God, the rule and reign of God in your everyday life. He shows you where God is ruling and where God and His Word are not yet ruling in your life. I have said many times that it will be sweet in the sweet by and by, but I must live in the nasty now and now. Many people in churches today have stopped at "I'm saved and one day I will go to Heaven," but God has more for those who are saved now.

*For John truly baptized with water; but ye shall be* ***baptized with the Holy Ghost*** *not many days hence* (Acts 1:5).

*Then remembered I the word of the Lord, how that he said, John indeed baptized with water; but ye* ***shall be baptized with the Holy Ghost*** (Acts 11:16). Baptized comes from the Greek word *"baptizo"—to dip, dye, immerse, initiate.* The

Holy Spirit is immersing, dipping, and initiating you into a totally new life, and you will never be the same again. The Holy Spirit takes you out of your old life and takes you with Him into the body of Christ.

The Apostle Paul writing to the Corinthians brings a clearer understanding of the work of baptism with the Holy Spirit. *For by one Spirit are we **all baptized into one body**, whether we be Jews or Gentiles, whether we be bond or free; and have been all made to drink into one Spirit* (1 Corinthians 12:13). The apostle explains that we are being baptized into the body of Christ. As you find new friends with the body of Christ, the family of God, you will spend less time with your old friends. There will come a time when you realize your old friends are not going the same way you're going now. You've been changed, you're different, and you don't want to do what they do anymore.

*For as many of you as have been **baptized into Christ** have put on Christ* (Galatians 3:27). I always remind people that Christ is not Jesus's last name. Christ in *Greek is Christos — The Messiah and the anointing, to rub with the oil of anointing and to consecrate.* The Holy Spirit is baptizing — *immersing and initiating* you into the anointing and clothing you with the anointing.

*Therefore, **if any man be in Christ, he is a new creature**: old things are passed away; behold, **all things are become new*** (2 Corinthians 5:17). When you get to this level and this work of the Holy Spirit when he puts you into the body of Christ, you have a new name, a new way of living, and a new purpose in life.

When you get up in the morning, it's not the old nine-to-five, dog-eat-dog, and try-to-get-to-the-top, the old way of life. When you get up in the morning now, you say, "What's the plan of God for me today? What's my body doing today, and what am I doing as a member of the body of Christ?" You are moving into Kingdom living, and this is an everyday new way of living. Do you want the Holy Spirit of God to do this with you?

## How the Holy Spirit Works in the Fourth Level of Faith—Receive

The apostle writes to the church at Ephesus and asks them a strange question.

*He said unto them,* **Have ye received the Holy Ghost since ye believed**? *And they said unto him, We have not so much as heard whether there be any Holy Ghost* (Acts 19:2). The Apostle Paul asked Christians at the church in Ephesus *"Have you received the Holy Spirit since you have believed?"* and they answered that they did not know *"whether there be any* Holy Ghost." Wait a minute. Of course, they knew the Holy Spirit because He was the one that brought salvation into their lives; they were already Christians and had experienced His work in their life. The Apostle Paul knew they believed and were saved, but was asking if they had received another level of the Holy Spirit working in their life since they believed. We can only understand what Paul is saying and the people's response by looking at the Greek word for receive, *"lambano,"* which means *to take hold deliberately by an act of your own will.* Because the church at Ephesus understood the Greek word for receive, they were astonished that this work of the Holy Spirit was available to them. They simply did not know they could have the Holy Spirit working in them daily.

Many preachers have asked, "Have you _received_ the _baptism_ of the Holy Spirit?" By combining and not differentiating the difference between baptism (salvation) and receiving (a daily walk), they miss out on the fantastic work the Holy Spirit desires to do in their life. Many in the church today have experienced the baptism or salvation work of the Holy Spirit but have yet to receive the Holy Spirit, where the Spirit lives in them each and every day. On Sunday, they feel the touch of the Holy Spirit, and their Faith is high, but when Monday comes, their Faith is low again. The problem is that they haven't received the Holy Spirit to live in them daily rather than it being just a weekend church thing.

*Howbeit when he, the Spirit of truth, is come,* **he will guide you into all truth***: for he shall not speak of himself; but whatsoever he shall hear, that shall he speak: and* **he will show you things to come** (John 16:13). As you receive the Holy Spirit, He becomes your helper, instructor, and mentor who will guide you in your ongoing maturing walk of Faith in the Kingdom of God. The Holy Spirit begins the process of producing the fruit of the Spirit in you. *But* **the fruit of the Spirit** *is love, joy, peace, longsuffering, gentleness, goodness, Faith, Meekness, temperance: against such, there is no law* (Galatians 5:22-23). Notice here that it is the fruit of "The Spirit" because He is now living in you. He produces the fruit that was impossible for you in your natural ability. He gives you the ability to love, have joy and peace that passes all understanding, to be able to walk in long-suffering toward others, to have the temperance to gain self-control. If you have tried to produce this fruit in your life and failed, you now know why; it can only be the work of the Spirit. As this fruit is produced, you become a witness to others, and they will see the difference in your life.

## How the Holy Spirit Works in the Fifth Level of Faith — Filled

This is when it really gets exciting! God fills us for service.

*And they were all **filled with the Holy Ghost**, and began to speak with other tongues, as the Spirit gave them utterance* (Acts 2:4). As always, it is essential to understand what the word *filled* means in Greek. The Greek word for filled is *"pleytho," meaning to fill, cram full, and be under the influence.* Just like when a person is under the influence of alcohol, their behavior changes — they speak differently and act boldly — when you are "under the influence" of the Holy Spirit, your behavior will also change, but under this influence, it is obviously for the better. When you're under the influence of the Holy Spirit, you will speak a new language, the language of Faith. Sometimes that language is unknown tongues, praying in the Spirit, or tongues that speak the "now" Word of God for that particular moment.

Just like being under the influence of alcohol wears off, being under the influence of the Holy Spirit also wears off. You could be at church and be under the influence of the Holy Spirit, and then get in your vehicle to go home and get into a disagreement with your spouse and be under a different influence very quickly. In a moment, you can go from Full of Faith to a half tank, and then by Monday morning, when the alarm goes off, you start your day under an entirely different influence.

The Apostle Paul gives the church at Ephesus great wisdom on how to be filled. *Wherefore be ye not unwise but understanding what the will of the Lord is. And be not drunk with wine, wherein is excess; but **be filled** with the Spirit; Speaking to yourselves in psalms and hymns and spiritual songs, singing and making melody in your heart to the Lord; Giving thanks always for all things unto God and the Father in the name of our Lord Jesus Christ* (Ephesians 5:17–20). Again, it is essential to return to Greek to understand the word "be filled." The word *be* in the aorist tense is to "be, being filled." It's not a one-time filling. Just like with the fleeting influence of alcohol, you'll need to drink again to get the effect of being under the influence of the Spirit. The Apostle Paul continues to explain how to be filled by speaking psalms, hymns, and spiritual songs, making melody in your heart and giving thanks. When you find yourself under influences other than the Spirit of God, begin to praise God, and the influence will come because *God inhabits the praises of His people* (Psalms 22:3).

As we are filled (under the influence), the Holy Spirit gives us "gifts" that enable us to be powerful witnesses for Him. We can see a list of motivational, ministry, and nine manifestation gifts we can expect as we are filled with the spirit.

*Now concerning **spiritual gifts**, brethren, I would not have you ignorant. Ye know that ye were Gentiles, carried away unto these dumb idols, even as ye were led. Wherefore I give you to understand that no man speaking by the Spirit of God calleth Jesus accursed: and that no man can say that Jesus is the Lord, but by the Holy Ghost. Now there are **diversities of gifts**, but the same Spirit. And there are **differences of***

***administrations,*** *but the same Lord.* ***And there are diversities of operations,*** *but it is the same God which worketh all in all* (1 Corinthians 12:1–6).

The diversities of gifts are the motivational gifts in you for serving, giving, exhorting, helping, and loving (Romans 5:4–15).

The administration gifts are ministry gifts of the apostle, prophet, evangelist, pastor, and teacher (Ephesians 4:8–12).

The operations are the manifestation gifts, the nine gifts of the Spirit (1 Corinthians 12:7–10).

*But the* ***manifestation of the Spirit is given to every man to profit withal.*** *For to one is given by the Spirit the* ***word of wisdom;*** *to another the* ***word of knowledge*** *by the same Spirit; To another* ***Faith*** *by the same Spirit; to another the* ***gifts of healing*** *by the same Spirit; To another the* ***working of miracles;*** *to another* ***prophecy;*** *to another* ***discerning of spirits;*** *to another* ***diverse kinds of tongues;*** *to another the* ***interpretation of tongues****: But all these worketh that one and the selfsame Spirit, dividing to every man severally as he will* (1 Corinthians 12:7–10).

I like to put the nine Gifts of the Spirit into three groups to explain them better.

- Power to Think. The Word of Knowledge, the Word of Wisdom, and the Discerning of Spirits give us the Power to Think the thoughts of God.
- Power to Speak. Tongues, interpretation of tongues, and prophecy give us the Power to Speak for God.

- Power to Act. The gifts of healing, the working of miracles, and the gift of Faith give us the Power to Act as God were to act.

All the gifts listed here are given to profit or help someone else. Remember, this is the Fifth Level of Faith, being Full of Faith to take the gospel to others. When God uses us in one of these gifts, we can expect the Word of God to increase, the number of disciples to multiply, priests to become obedient to the Faith, and wonders and miracles to happen among the people. A foundation verse for Level Five was: *And the saying pleased the whole multitude: and they chose Stephen,* ***a man FULL OF FAITH*** *and of the Holy Ghost, and Philip, and Prochorus, and Nicanor, and Timon, and Parmenas, and Nicolas a proselyte of Antioch: Whom they set before the apostles: and when they had prayed, they laid their hands on them. And* ***the word of God increased****; and the number of the* ***disciples multiplied*** *in Jerusalem greatly; and a great company of* ***the priests were obedient to the Faith****. And Stephen,* ***full of Faith and power****, did great wonders and* ***miracles*** *among the people* (Acts 6:5–8).

## The Holy Spirit Works to Give You the Power to Be His Witness

***But ye shall receive power, after that the Holy Ghost is come upon you: and ye shall be witnesses*** *unto me both in Jerusalem, and in all Judaea, and in Samaria, and unto the uttermost part of the earth (Acts 1:8).*

*And he said unto them,* ***Go ye into all the world, and preach*** *the gospel to every creature. He that believeth and is baptized shall be saved; but he that believeth not shall be damned. And* *these signs shall follow them that believe; In my name shall they cast out Devils; they shall speak with new tongues; They shall take up serpents; and if they drink any deadly thing, it shall not hurt them; they shall lay hands on the sick, and they shall recover* (Mark 16:15–18).

*And* **this gospel of the kingdom shall be preached in all the world for a witness** *unto all nations; and then shall the end come* (Matthew 24:14).

Now that you have the Holy Spirit working in you in The Five Levels of Faith, go into all the world with the Power to Think, the Power to Speak, and the Power to Act to witness His power.

## Questions:

- How does the Holy Spirit work in the First level of Faith?
- How does the Holy Spirit work in the Second level of Faith?
- How does the Holy Spirit work in the Third level of Faith?
- How does the Holy Spirit work in the Fourth level of Faith?
- How does the Holy Spirit work in the Fifth level of Faith?
- What are the nine gifts of the Holy Spirit?
- Why do many sound like tinkling cymbals or sounding brass?

- Why do you need to "be being" filled?
- Why do you need to be filled to go and preach the gospel?

# Prayer Focus:

- Pray that you will recognize the working of the Holy Spirit in each level of Faith.
- Pray that you will discern the difference between the administrative gifts and the gifts of the spirit to witness.
- Pray for the Holy Spirit to come upon you to be a witness.
- Pray that you will understand the three gifts to think.
- Pray that you will understand the three gifts to speak.
- Pray that you will understand the three gifts to act.
- Pray that you will recognize when you are only a tinkling cymbal and sounding brass.
- Pray that you will continue to "be being filled" with the Spirit.
- Pray that you will discern what "influence" you are under during the day.
- Pray that your actions will demonstrate your Faith and bring attention to God, not yourself.
- Pray that you will continue speaking to yourself in psalms, hymns, spiritual songs, and thankfulness in your heart, so you are in a position to be filled.
- Pray that the Lord will begin to use you in the gifts of the Spirit to be a witness.

# CHAPTER 9

# Demons and The Three Aspects of Faith

As we begin this chapter, please read this confession aloud: *"I can have everything the Bible says I can have, I can be everything the Bible says I can be, and I can do everything the Bible says I can do. Today I'm going to let the Word become life in my life."*

## Principalities, Powers, Rulers, Wicked Spirits

*For we wrestle not against flesh and blood, but against **principalities**, against **powers**, against the **rulers** of the darkness of this world, against spiritual **wickedness** in high places* (Ephesians 6:12). The Apostle Paul begins with what we should not be wrestling against, which is precisely what many people wrestle with most of the time. We are supposed to be in a fight of Faith, not a fight of flesh, and yet we fight to get out of bed in the morning, fight to discipline what we eat or what we listen to, and fight with family members without ever having made it to the actual fight yet.

A real battle is going on in the spirit realm, and we need to be aware of demons working to steal and hinder our Faith. Apostle Paul gives us a list and brilliantly puts the demons in four categories for us to understand easily. The categories are principalities, powers, rulers, and wicked spirits in high places. The study of demonology is inexhaustible, as you can find different names of these demons in scripture — unclean spirits, foul spirits, legion, spirits of infirmity, deaf and dumb spirits, perverse spirits, lying spirits, spirits of fear — and the list goes on.

With so many demon names out there, I have written a complete syllabus on this that can help identify which specific demon you may be dealing with. Still, I have found that many people get caught up with this and get in the ditch, wanting to know more about demons and their names than the power of God to gain victory over them.

Some people get off in the ditch with the study of demons. They think if they know the demon's name, they can get rid of it. I submit to you that I can get rid of demons whether I know their name or not, just like I can get rid of a telemarketer on the phone whether I know their name or not.

But it is helpful to at least know the Greek meaning for each of the four categories of demons and learn how they operate in the world.

**Principalities** — *Greek: arche* — *The highest rank in order of commencement, in order of time and rank, precedence, chief.* The practical application would be Satan and the one-third of the fallen angels (Revelation 12:4). The next order would be the Antichrist and the world rulers. The Devil is the father of lies, looking for people to work and speak through, so he begins to set up his process of influence and deception.

**Powers**—*Greek: exousia*—*Delegated influence, authority to act on one's behalf, jurisdiction according to the ability to gain control.* The practical application would be that the Devil assigns demons to influence those who have delegated authority, such as world dictators, presidents, and governors who have a position of influence that affects people in entire countries.

**Rulers**—*Greek: kosmokrator*—*World rulers, to carry off, orderly arrangement affecting its inhabitants, morally, provide, obtain.* The practical application is seen in society's seven mountains of influence: **religion, family, education, government, media, arts and entertainment, and business.** At one time, the church held the influence of all these mountains of influence. The education mountain of influence was felt at every level, from grade school to college. Many of the original presidents at the Ivy League schools were pastors, and the institutions initially started out with training ministers to preach the gospel. Government officials would lay their hand on the Bible and commit to leading the nation as one nation under God.

As you can see, each mountain has undergone cultural change, and it's almost impossible to find the Bible and God as the foundational influence now. True to the definition of this rank of rulers, we can see the organized rule over societies creating unique spiritual atmospheres influencing society's inhabitants. They are all working together to hold groups of people in bondage.

**Wickedness—Greek: pomeria**—*hurtful words, the depravity of character, malice, plots, sins, iniquity, degeneracy of virtue, mischief, and evil.* The practical application of this is evil words and thoughts in high places— your mind, will, and emotions. Wickedness is *evil* words to keep you from letting the Word become life in your life. These evil words of influence ultimately produce divorce, addictions, pride, guilt, depression, deceit, lust, and fear. I was the guest speaker at a pastors' conference, and some of the pastors told me they had rented an airplane to fly over the city to cast down wicked spirits in "high places." They said one of those spirits was the spirit of adultery that was influencing many in their churches. I told them I had been in many cities that had different predominant spirits over them, but I did not immediately commit adultery or become a meth addict. I explained that these "high" places that need to be dealt with are in people's minds, where these evil words influence people. When you change a person's mind with the Word of God, they will be free from any spirit over the city.

Understanding the four categories has helped me a few times. A few months ago, one of my ministers who had been dealing with sickness and pain came to our conference. Even though he believed in God for the promise of healing, he had others pray for him, but there had been no change. He came to the altar and requested I pray for him. As I was about to lay hands on him for healing, the Lord showed me the problem was a spirit of infirmity. I took authority over the spirit, cast it out, and in a few minutes, he started walking and running around the sanctuary, completely healed. I talked with him recently, and he is still healed, so we can learn from this that sometimes we need healing, and other times we must deal with a spirit.

The study of demonology also includes the levels of possession—depression, oppression, suppression, obsession, and possession. There is a process the Devil uses to gain more access to your life. He starts with depression. If you're depressed, you're on your way to the other levels. Next comes the medicine for depression, which ultimately brings side effects, and the problem worsens; there is a better way.

I have experienced many demon manifestations in my forty years of ministry. I've seen distorted bodies slithering on the floor, people arching up, their eyeballs rolling back in their heads, teeth beginning to distort into sharp points in their mouths, and some with incredible supernatural strength. And I've heard voices that were not human coming out of people, but all of them were set free in a matter of moments.

One time in my bedroom, two demons were on top of me like monkeys. One was holding my mouth, and I couldn't breathe; the other was holding my legs, and I couldn't move. I felt paralyzed. I thought I was a goner. I tried to say Jesus's name, but the spirit had his hand right over my mouth, and I couldn't even speak. I finally mumbled the name Jesus, and they were gone when I did. Another time, I was staying in my trailer house. The ceiling was not that tall, but this giant demon was standing in the corner of the doorway with his head bent over because he was taller than the ceiling. The room became cold as ice. It could have been snowing in there, it was so cold. After I gained my senses, I rebuked him, and he left. I've seen enough demons in my life to last me for a lifetime, and I'm not interested in seeing any more. I want you to know, that, even if you think you want to see one, you don't. Just relax and enjoy life without that experience. I've cast many demons, so I understand all this other teaching about demonology. I can go through all the obsession, possession, and suppression, but I want to talk to you today about overcoming all of them in three easy steps. How's that sound?

We have learned that the four categories of demons, each with their rank and position, have one main goal and work together to influence every inhabitant of the Earth with evil words. The only way to wrestle with these spirits is with Faith and the Word of God by letting the Word become life in our life.

I don't care what their name is. I don't care what progression it is. I don't even care what rank it is. I've learned that you can overcome every one of them in three easy steps, called the Three Aspects of Faith.

Jesus demonstrated the process of systematically overcoming demons by using the Three Aspects of Faith.

# Three Temptations of Jesus

*Then was Jesus led up of the Spirit into the **wilderness** to be **tempted** of the Devil* (Matthew 4:1). God does not tempt us; however, He will lead us through life and allow the temptations of the enemy to try us to see if we will use our Faith. The enemy will first come when we are in the wilderness, a lonely dry place. We are more susceptible to his temptations when we are alone without the support of others. Have you ever felt dry and aggravated some days? Be aware that is a time the enemy will try you.

*And when he had fasted forty days and forty nights, he was afterward an hungred* (Matthew 4:2). The second time temptation will come is when we're hungry. The enemy knows you will eat just about anything if you're hungry. Maybe you've been trying to eat right, on a strict diet, but you are at work or on the road, and fast food is the only thing available — and there goes your diet out the window. Similarly, the enemy knows when you're spiritually hungry — He can try to tempt you with something sweet that is not the Word of God.

*Blessed are they which do **hunger** and **thirst after righteousness**: for they shall be filled* (Matthew 5:6). We need to develop a deep hunger for being in the right standing with God. I remember my mom saying, "I've got a hankering for a piece of pie, a pickle, or a pizza." I was unsure if hankering was an accurate word, but in the dictionary, it is an old word used to denote a strong desire, longing, or craving for something. Hankering comes from middle Dutch *hangen*, to hang on until you get something. If you're hankering for something, you'll do whatever it takes to get it. How much more should we hunger and crave the Word of God, read, study, and dig through the scriptures until we're satisfied? This kind of hunger is much more than just a quick snack in a Sunday church service. How hungry are you, and what are you hungry for?

***The thief** cometh not, but for to **steal**, and to **kill**, and to **destroy**: I am come that they might have life, and that they might have it more abundantly* (John 10:10). One day, when I was reading this verse, I got so excited that I ran around my living room shouting, "Yes, the Devil is coming to steal from me." You're probably wondering why I would be excited about the Devil coming to steal from me. Well, if the Devil is coming to steal from me, that means I have something so valuable the Devil himself wants it. I'm not struggling to get the promise of God. I already have it by His Grace through Faith; the Devil is simply trying to take it from me. This revelation changed my whole Faith walk. The Devil tries in three ways: First, to steal and take what's yours when you're not looking or aware of it. Second, to kill or trick you into sacrificing it or giving it up, or simply giving up. The third is to destroy, mar, ruin, or tarnish your testimony. I've given the example of a beautiful wood pulpit at the front of the sanctuary that you scratch a swear word on with a sharp instrument. How could you preach the Word of God with people looking at a swear word on the pulpit? The pulpit would be marred or ruined for its purpose. If the Devil can't steal our Faith and get us to give up our Faith, he'll try to mar our testimony, which is ruined. Some preachers have destroyed their testimony and name. People can't see past their marred testimony, even though they may still have the Word and be able to preach well.

## Temptations Come in Three Areas

*Love not the world, neither the things that are in the world. If any man love the world, the love of the Father is not in him. For all that is in the world,* **the lust of the flesh***, and* **the lust of the eyes***, and* **the pride of life***, is not of the Father, but is of the world. And the world passeth away, and the lust thereof: but* **he that doeth the will of God** *abideth forever* (1 John 2:15–17).

- Lust of the Flesh — provision, health
- Lust of the Eyes — pride, quick recognition, self-centered desires
- Pride of Life — Desire to attain excess greatness or power without God

## The Lust of the Flesh — Provision, Health

*And when the tempter came to him, he said, If thou be the Son of God,* **command that these stones be made bread** (Matthew 4:3). When the tempter came to Jesus, he went with an "if" question to instill doubt, meaning to say it's a possibility that you believe who you are, but if you are the son of God like you think you are, then prove it by commanding these stones to be made bread. The same temptation will come to you in the same way. If you're really a pastor, if you're really an elder, if you're really a prophet, if you're really a believer, if you're really a Christian, then use your Faith to do it for yourself for your own provision. The first temptation is tricky. Am I going to use my Faith for my provision, to benefit myself, or did my Heavenly Father promise that He would take care of me?

*Jesus handled this by answering and saying,* ***It is written****, Man shall not live by bread alone, but by every word that proceedeth out of the mouth of God* (Matthew 4:4).

*So we can see that Jesus applied the first aspect of Faith — The Word of Faith — by hearing the message of God.*

Jesus knew what God said about how bread, health, and physical well-being are taken care of and is a provision of The Word of Faith, the first Aspect of Faith. We must know the promises of God when we find ourselves in temptation.

Jesus quoted the exact scripture concerning the temptation of provision for himself. Notice Jesus did not react to the temptation of proving He was the Son of God; He simply said what His Father said, giving glory to God.

## The Lust of the Eyes — Pride, Quick Recognition, Self-centered Desire

*Then the Devil taketh him up into the holy city, and setteth him on a pinnacle of the temple, And saith unto him,* ***If thou be the Son of God, cast thyself down****: for it is written, He shall give his angels charge concerning thee: and in their hands they shall bear thee up, lest at any time thou dash thy foot against a stone. Jesus said unto him,* ***It is written*** *again, Thou shalt not tempt the Lord thy God* (Matthew 4:5–7).

The Devil comes in this second temptation with an "if" question like before, but this time, he starts quoting scripture out of context to trick Jesus. The first temptation was about flesh and survival, but now this temptation has to do with our soul, mind, will, and emotions. OK, Jesus, if you're so spiritual quoting scripture, why don't you do some wild supernatural thing so you can draw a crowd and a following quickly? Will you use your Faith to show off to get quick recognition? Many will fall for this and want to act super spiritual to impress people for their immediate recognition. What did Jesus do? He just goes back to Faith in the Word for the answer.

*Jesus said unto him,* ***It is written*** *again, Thou shalt not tempt the Lord thy God* (Matthew 4:7).

Jesus applies the First Aspect of Faith — The Word of Faith, hearing the message of God — to what God did about this proposition. He uses the Second Aspect of Faith — The Law of Faith, obeying and applying — by saying that jumping off the temple would be tempting God, which is against The Law of Faith. The answer to the temptation is The Word of Faith and The Law of Faith; that's it, that simple, no-drawn-out fight with the Devil. Are you starting to see that wrestling with the Devil is easier than it sounds?

## The Pride of Life—Desire to Attain Excess Greatness or Power Without God

*Again, the Devil taketh him up into an exceeding high mountain, and sheweth him **all the kingdoms of the world, and the glory of them;** And saith unto him, **All these things will I give thee, if thou wilt fall down and worship me*** (Matthew 4:8–9).

The Devil comes again and uses an "if" each time. But this time, he changes the focus to himself as the answer for the provision. The temptations have been progressive: the flesh, the soul, and the spirit. You are a spirit; you possess a soul and live in a house called a body. Thus, these temptations have come in each aspect of our being (1 Thessalonians 5:23). Our spirit is whom we are created to be and our purpose in life. The Devil is after getting control of it. If you surrender to him, he will offer the world and all its splendor. The Devil will provide everybody a shortcut to fame, but the way with God will prove much better; wait for it.

The Devil takes Jesus to an exceedingly high mountain and shows him the "kingdoms" of the world. What were they? The seven mountains of influence in society: *religion, family, education, government, media, arts and entertainment, and business*. The exceedingly high mountain is his ranks and categories of spirits: *principalities, powers, rulers, and wicked spirits* over the seven mountains. The Devil's offer to Jesus is that he will set you above all of them if you worship him. The Devil's temptation is powerful here because the purpose of Jesus was to be seated above all principality, power, might, and dominion and to have all things under his feet (Ephesians 2:18–22). I am saddened to have known pastor friends who sold out for quick fame and eventually went shipwreck. They went from immediate fame to not even being in the ministry today. How will you keep from being deceived, the same way Jesus did by using the Three Aspects of Faith?

*Then saith Jesus unto him, Get thee hence, Satan: for **it is written**, Thou shalt worship the Lord thy God, and him only shalt thou serve. Then the Devil leaveth him, and behold, angels came and ministered unto him* (Matthew 4:10–11).

Jesus overcomes by using the Three Aspects of Faith in order: The Word of Faith—hearing the message of God (it is written), The Law of Faith—worship and obedience, and The Spirit of Faith—serve. Immediately after beating the three temptations, God sent angels, and they ministered to Him. Ministered in the **Greek—*diakoneo*—** *to wait as a host, set the table, serve as an attendant, and run errands*. God will supernaturally reward you when you overcome temptation with your Faith.

*And Jesus being **full** of the Holy Ghost, returned from Jordan and was **led** by the Spirit into the wilderness, Being forty days **tempted of the Devil**. And **Jesus returned in the power of the Spirit** into Galilee: and there went out **a fame of him** through all the region round about* (Luke 4:1–14).

Jesus went into the temptations Full of Faith after His baptism in the Jordan. He passed the tests, came out of the temptations full of power, and qualified for ministry. Jesus became famous not because of compromise, prideful acts, or a shortcut but through obedience to His Heavenly Father. He became famous by saying no to fame.

## Jesus Begins a Powerful Time of Ministry

*And **he taught in their synagogues**, being glorified of all. And he came to Nazareth, where he had been brought up: and, as his custom was, he went into the synagogue on the Sabbath day, and stood up for to read. And there was delivered unto him the book of the prophet Esaias. And **when he had opened the book, he found the place where it was written, The Spirit of the Lord is upon me**, because he hath **anointed me to preach** the gospel to the poor; he hath sent me **to heal** the brokenhearted, to preach **deliverance** to the captives, and **recovering of sight** to the blind, to set at **liberty** them that are bruised, To **preach** the acceptable year of the Lord* (Luke 4:15–19).

Jesus opened the scriptures and found His purpose in Isaiah 61:1–2, which just happened to be the reading portion of the Torah that day. After Jesus finished reading and sat down, others began to stare at him because they knew this scripture had never been read with such power and anointing. Jesus responds, *"This day, this scripture is fulfilled in your ears"* (Luke 4:21).

- Do you want to pass the tests of the Devil's temptation and come out with power?
- Do you want the Spirit of the Lord upon you to minister to others?

- Are you ready to engage in a powerful time for your ministry?

Now that you know how to overcome temptations, you can find your purpose in scripture. You can say, the Spirit of the Lord is upon me and anointed me to preach, heal, deliver, and set them that are bound at liberty. You can say today, this scripture is fulfilled in my life. You can say, I let the Word become life in my life.

## Questions:

- What are the four levels of the demonic that we wrestle with?
- What is your level of hunger and thirst for the righteousness of God?
- What was the first temptation Jesus faced?
- What was the second temptation Jesus faced?
- What was the third temptation Jesus faced?
- How did Jesus overcome each temptation?
- How did Jesus use the Three Aspects of Faith in each temptation?
- Why did Jesus need to be Full of Faith to face the temptations?
- Why did Jesus come out of the temptations full of power?
- Jesus was full of power for what kind of ministry?

## Prayer Focus:

- Pray that you will recognize and understand the levels of demonic influence that are active in the world today.
- Pray for the gut-wrenching hunger and thirst for the righteousness of God.
- Pray that you will discern when the Lust of the Flesh tempts you.
- Pray that you will discern when the Lust of the Eyes tempts you.
- Pray that you discern when your pride in life tempts you.
- Pray that you will understand how to apply the Three Aspects of Faith to overcome.
- Pray that you will increase to the level of Full of Faith to face the temptations.
- Pray that you will recognize the only way to overcome temptation is with "it is written."
- Pray that you will increase to full Faith to overcome temptations and be counted worthy of the Power of the Spirit to be a witness.
- Pray that your actions will demonstrate your Faith and bring attention to God, not yourself.
- Pray that you understand that ministry is about improving someone else's life.
- Pray that the Lord will begin to use you in the gifts of the Spirit to be a witness.

# CHAPTER 10

# Faith Scatters the Enemies

As we begin this chapter, please read this confession aloud: *"I can have everything the Bible says I can have, I can be everything the Bible says I can be, and I can do everything the Bible says I can do. Today I'm going to let the Word become life in my life."*

## Let God Arise

***Let God arise, let his enemies be scattered*** (Psalm 68:1).

*When the men were come unto him, they said,* ***John Baptist hath sent us*** *unto thee, saying,* ***Art thou he that should come? or do we look for another?*** *And in* ***that same hour he cured many of their infirmities and plagues****, and of* ***evil spirits****, and unto many that* ***were blind he gave sight****. Then Jesus answering said unto them, Go your way, and tell John what things ye have seen and heard; how that* ***the blind see, the lame walk, the lepers are cleansed, the deaf hear, the dead are raised, to the poor, the gospel is preached*** (Luke 7:20–22).

The Apostle John is inquiring whether Jesus is the Messiah to come because, when he baptized Jesus, he saw the Spirit of God come upon Him. Jesus returns the answer to John's question by stating the works of God that He was doing. Jesus also made it clear that the works He was doing were not of himself, but the Father in Him was doing them (John 14:10). God was arising through His Son doing the works.

## Who Are the Enemies of God?

- **Blindness**—*Inability to See*
- **Lameness**—*Inability to Walk*
- **Sickness**—*Inability to Act*
- **Deafness**—*Inability to Hear*
- **Deadness**—*Inability to Respond*
- **Slackness**—*Inability to Contribute*

*Moses listed the enemies of God: And the LORD said unto Moses, Speak unto the priests the sons of Aaron, and say unto them, For whatsoever man he be that hath a blemish (physical or moral spot), he shall not approach: a blind man, or a lame, or he that hath a flat nose, or anything superfluous, Or a man that is broken footed, or broken handed, Or crookbacked, or a dwarf, or that hath a blemish in his eye, or be scurvy, or scabbed, or hath his stones broken; No man that hath a blemish of the seed of Aaron the priest shall come nigh to offer the offerings of the LORD made by fire: he hath a blemish; he shall not come nigh to offer the bread of his God. He shall eat the bread of his God, both of the most holy, and of the holy. Only he shall not go in unto the vail, nor come nigh unto the altar, because he hath a blemish; that he profane not my sanctuaries: for I the LORD do sanctify them* (Leviticus 21:1–23).

Moses speaks to the priests and gives them a list of those who are disqualified to stand in the holy place. The Lord told Moses that those with these blemishes would profane His sanctuary by not representing God well. We could study the Hebrew word for each of the blemishes listed here, but they are the six enemies of God that I've been discussing. If the priests have not overcome the enemies, how can they help others overcome them?

I love how Jesus sums it all up with one thought-provoking question, *And he spake a parable unto them,* **Can the blind lead the blind?** *Shall they not* **both fall into the ditch?** (Luke 6:39). If we continue with the idea of this parable, we could ask questions for each of the enemies.

- **Can the blind lead anyone?**
- **Can the lame lead an army?**
- **Can the deaf speak clear words from God?**
- **Can the sick heal anyone?**
- **Can the dead give life?**
- **Can the poor preach the gospel?**

We would have to say no to each of the questions in our own strength, but the good news is through Faith, we can let God arise in us and scatter each of His enemies. *Let God arise; let his enemies be scattered* (Psalm 68:1).

Yes, Jesus can scatter the enemies of God, the physical, the spiritual, the mental, and the moral enemies; all of these keep people from God's life and purpose for them. The enemies are working to keep you from doing what God called you to do and to keep you from being what God has intended for you. God has an excellent plan for your life and desires to scatter the enemies that keep you from that plan.

We can see all throughout scripture that Jesus can scatter these enemies.

- **Jesus healed the physically blind**: (Matthew 11:5, Matthew 12:22, Matthew 15:30–31, Matthew 20:30–34, Matthew 21:14, Matthew 9:27–31, Mark 8:22–25, Mark 10:46–52, Luke 4:18, Luke 18:35, John 5:3, John 9:1–2, John 9:6–25, John 9:32).

- **Jesus ministers to the spiritually and mentally blind**: (Isaiah 42:19, Isaiah 43:8, Isaiah 56:10, Isaiah 59:10, Matthew 15:14, Matthew 23:16, Matthew 23:17–19, Matthew 23:24–26, Luke 6:39, John 9:39–41, Romans 2:19, 2 Peter 1:9, Revelation 3:17)

- **Jesus and the Apostles healed the physically lame**: (Matthew 11:5, Matthew 15:30–31, Matthew 21:14, Luke 7:22, Acts 3:2–11, Acts 8:7, Acts 14:8–10)

- **Ministry and healing to the spiritually and mentally lame**: (Proverbs 26:7, Malachi 1:13)

- **Ministry and healing to the physically sick**: (Matthew 10:7–8, 2 Kings 7:8, Matthew 11:5, Luke 4:27, Luke 17:12–19)

- **Ministry and healing to the spiritually and mentally sick**: (Romans 12:1, Ephesians 4:17–22, Philippians 2:5, Hebrews 8:10)

- **Ministry and healing to the physically deaf**: (Luke 7:20)
- **Ministry and healing to the spiritually and mentally deaf**: (Psalms 38:13, Psalms 58:4, Isaiah 42:18–19, Isaiah 43:8, Isaiah 29:18, Isaiah 35:5)
- **Ministry and raising the physically dead**: (John 11:21–43, Acts 9:36–41)
- **Ministry and raising the spiritually and mentally dead**: (Matthew 23:27–28, Psalm 115:17; James 2:17–20)
- **The gospel preached to the physically poor**: (Mark 14:7, Deuteronomy 15:11, Psalm 10:9)
- **The gospel preached to the spiritually and mentally poor**: (Judges 6:15, Matthew 17:16, Mark 9:18, Luke 20:33–7, John 12:37–40, Hebrews 3:19, 2 Timothy 4:3)

# Faith Can Scatter the Six Enemies of God

You are not going to scatter the enemies of God with your ability alone or just because the Spirit of God dwells in you, but when God arises in you, the attention of everyone in the room will see your Faith as God scatters His enemies through you. When God in you scatters the enemies in your life, they will have confidence that the enemies in their life can also be scattered. Remember, it is not you who does the work; the Father in you is doing it. Your Faith in His Word and Law allows Him to accomplish His work in and through you.

**When the enemies of God are shattered (broken and smashed to pieces),** people are set free from their enemies:

physical, spiritual, mental, and moral enemies that keep people from the life and purpose of God.

You can use your Faith to receive God's help in shattering the enemy. Or you could just make excuses.

**The Top Ten Lame Excuses in the Bible**

#10: The snake made me do it (Eve)

#9: The woman you gave to me made me do it (Adam)

#8: I would have died if I hadn't eaten some of that red stuff (Esau)

#7: The rivers back home are cleaner (Naaman)

#6: My family "ain't" much to speak of (Gideon)

#5: I don't speak so "good" (Moses)

#4: It's only a few (bleating) animals (Saul)

#3: I'm too young (Jeremiah)

#2: Gotta bury my father first (Person-Jesus-called)

**And What is the #1 Lamest Excuse in the Bible** *(in my opinion)?*

#1: "I threw the gold into the fire, and out came a golden calf!" (Aaron)

**Without a strong faith, the enemy can attack you with all the enemies of God.**

- **Has the enemy of blindness kept you from seeing the Word of God?** Many have asked me, "How did you see that in that scripture? I've read that verse five times but never saw what you brought out in that scripture." I always replied, "He opened my mind to understand the scripture" (Luke 24:45). As you read His Word, ask God to reveal and help you see and understand what He is saying.

- **Has the enemy of deafness kept you from hearing God's voice?** Hearing and not hearing (Matthew 13:12). God speaks to His people in His Word, preaching, dreams, and many other ways. I've had people come to me to interpret their dreams. Often, they're frustrated and have asked why God doesn't just make it plain so they can hear what He is saying to them if He wants to speak to them? After I interpret their dream, they will often say that, in hindsight, the meaning was obvious. You can scatter this enemy by Faith, knowing it's God's will for you to hear His voice.

- **Has the enemy of lameness kept you from walking in Faith?** I hope you enjoyed the top ten lame excuses of those in the Bible. This enemy will use almost anything to keep you from walking out of your Faith. I can't go to church because I'm tired. I didn't sleep well last night, I'm too tired; I don't feel well; I just can't do this — and the list goes on. Stop the excuses, get up in Faith, and just start walking and scatter the enemy.

- **Has the enemy of sickness kept you from acting in Faith?** I remember a time when I was scheduled to teach a Sunday School class, and I was sick. I had the choice to cancel or teach. So, I chose to teach about healing, and by the time I was done teaching, I was completely healed! Several years ago, I took a young man who I was training in the ministry to Peru with me on a mission trip. I scheduled him to preach, but he got sick with the food he ate and told me he couldn't preach because he was throwing up. I told him he had to preach anyway and to trust me. At the end of his message, he prayed for three sick people, and they were healed on the spot. He came to me afterward and said, "I hated you for making me preach, but now I want to thank you for training me on how Faith works." I told him that if you don't learn how to scatter the enemy in this situation, the enemy will use this same tactic to keep him from ministering to others. Remember, Great Faith is when you use your Faith for someone else's needs.

- **Has the enemy of deadness kept you from the ability to respond?** The best way to recognize when the enemy of deadness comes to you is when you hear yourself saying, "I just don't feel anything, and I just don't have any enthusiasm." This is the perfect time to begin to praise the Lord! The scripture says, *"The dead praise not the Lord"* (Psalm 115:17). The physically dead obviously do not praise the Lord, but the spiritually and mentally dead are not praising Him either. God inhabits the praises of His people (Psalm 22:3). If you need to feel God and need some enthusiasm, rise up in Faith and offer the sacrifice of praise to the Lord (Hebrews 13:15).

- **Has the enemy of slackness kept you from giving or contributing?** You can recognize this enemy when you think you have nothing to offer. Whether physical or spiritual, it comes from a poor mindset. I often give this acronym for poor—P.O.O.R.—Passed Over

**O**pportunities **R**epeatedly. God will give everybody opportunities to contribute something. He would not give you the opportunity if He did not know that you had something to contribute. *As we have therefore opportunity, let us do good unto all men* (Galatians 6:10). Start with giving your time, a helping hand, a kind word, a prayer, or a word of encouragement, and you will be surprised what God will do through you. *Silver and gold have I none; but such as I have give I thee* (Acts 3:6). Whatever you put your hand to will prosper (Deuteronomy 28).

# As You Go

*Once you have recognized how the enemy has been attacking you, you can arise up as you go.*

***And as ye go****, preach, saying, The kingdom of Heaven is at hand. Heal the sick, cleanse the lepers, raise the dead, cast out Devils: freely ye have received, freely give* (Matthew 10:7–8).

As you go to church, as you go through your week, as you go to your job, as you go to the grocery store, and wherever you go, preach and expect God to arise and scatter His enemies. When the thought "I can't do this" comes, remember it is not *you* who can do it but God arising in you who can and will do it. Freely as you have received, freely give.

*Therefore, those who were scattered went everywhere preaching the word. Then Philip went down to the city of Samaria and preached Christ to them. And the multitudes with one accord heeded the things spoken by Philip, hearing and seeing the miracles which he did* (Acts 8:4–6).

They went everywhere and preached the Word; they let the Word become life in their life. Decide today to make preaching and scattering the enemies of God a lifestyle.

*Then said Jesus to them again, Peace be unto you:* **as my Father hath sent me, even so send I you.** *And when he had said this, he* **breathed** *on them, and saith unto them,* **Receive ye the Holy Ghost** (John 20:21–22).

The Father sent Jesus to scatter His enemies, and now He is sending you. This is the time to apply the Three Aspects of Faith: The Word of Faith that God is sending you, The Law of Faith is God giving you the right to go in His name, and The Spirit of Faith, Jesus, is giving you the same power of the Spirit that He used to scatter the enemies. Remember from a previous chapter how the Holy Spirit works with you in each level of Faith.

*Verily, verily, I say unto you,* **He that believeth on me, the works that I do shall he do also;** *and* **greater works than these shall he do,** *because I go unto my Father* (John 14:12).

Jesus is saying verily, verily, truthfully, truthfully, this is absolutely the truth; please pay attention. For you to believe this, you must apply The Law of Faith. He is giving you the legal right to do the same works He did, which was to scatter the enemies of God. Jesus is going to the Father, so it is your turn now to continue the work.

Let the Word become life in your life.

## Questions:

- How will we know when God arises?
- What are the six main enemies of God?
- How will you know when an enemy of God is scattered?
- Do you want God to arise in you to scatter the enemies of God?
- Why must we first be free from the enemies of God to scatter them in others?
- Can the blind lead anyone? Why not?
- Can the lame lead an army? Why not?
- Can the deaf speak clear words from God? Why not?
- Can the sick heal anyone? Why not?
- Can the dead give life? Why not?
- Can the poor preach the gospel? Why not?

## Prayer Focus:

- Pray that God will arise and scatter the enemies today.
- Pray that God will arise in you to scatter the enemies.
- Pray that you will discern the six main enemies of God.
- Pray that you will discern which enemy you have not scattered in your life yet.
- Pray that your blindness will be healed so you can help others to see.
- Pray that your lameness will be healed so you can help others to walk.

- Pray that your sickness will be healed so you can help others to act.

- Pray that your deafness will be healed so you can help others to hear.

- Pray that your deadness will be healed so you can help others to respond.

- Pray that your slackness will be healed so you can help others to contribute.

- Pray that you will apply the Three Aspects of Faith daily.

- Pray that you will continue to increase your Level of Faith.

- Pray that you will daily walk through the Process of Faith.

- Pray that you will always apply The Law of Faith.

- Pray that you will Keep the Faith.

- Pray that you will allow the Holy Spirit in the Five Levels of your Faith.

- Pray that you will defeat the demons in each Level of your Faith.

- Pray that Faith arises in you to scatter the enemies of God wherever you go.

- Pray that you will "let the Word become life in your life!"

# CHAPTER 11

# The Communication of Your Faith

As we begin this chapter, please read this confession out loud: *"I can have everything the Bible says I can have, I can be everything the Bible says I can be, and I can do everything the Bible says I can do. Today I'm going to let the Word become life in my life."*

Humankind has been trying to master the art of communication throughout the ages. They began with every means available, painting on cave walls, sending smoke signals, chiseling on stone tablets, writing on parchment, and using carrier pigeons. They advanced to telegraph, newspapers, magazines, radio, telephone, pagers, TV, snail mail, letters, books, and video. Today we have email, social media, cell phones, and text messages. We must ask ourselves whether we are any more effective in our communication or whether a flood of information caused people to be numb and disinterested. People have become numb to the flood of communication because they know much of the communication is designed only to benefit the communicator and has no benefit for them.

*That **the communication of thy Faith** may **become effectual** by the **acknowledging** of every good thing which is **in you in Christ Jesus*** (Philemon 6).

Philemon makes a powerful statement explaining how communication causes our Faith to become effective. If we look at the word *communication* in its **Greek form, koinonia**—*partnership, participation, social intercourse (words as seed producing a harvest), communion, sharing, distribution, fellowship* — we see that Philemon is praying that participating in and sharing your Faith may produce and promote full recognition, appreciation, understanding, and precise knowledge of every good thing in your identification with Christ Jesus and unto His glory.

For your Faith to become effective, you must get it from your heart and into your mouth. As you speak your Faith, it becomes a supernatural seed that produces a harvest not only in your life but in the lives of others. As you acknowledge every good thing that is in you in Christ Jesus, you partner with God to bring forth the harvest that God desires for your life, bringing glory back to God. If your Faith is to become effective, you must communicate it.

Some people talk constantly; if you try to say something, they just keep talking. I'm unsure whether they have any purpose in their communication other than just enjoying hearing themselves talk. How much communication has the purpose of Faith to become effective in not only our lives but in the lives of others?

Communication should promote full recognition, appreciation, understanding, and precise knowledge of the promises of God that will produce a harvest. As a communicator, I partner with God as a companion, associate, and distributor of His precious seed that will cause Faith to become effective in the hearer. Communicating your Faith in salvation and healing will produce salvation and healing, as with every good thing in you in Christ Jesus. No communication, no effect. As we have learned, Faith cannot be general but needs to be precise. You will not have healing because you just believe Jesus loves you; you must be precise that with His stripes, you were healed, which is The Law of Faith, and then your Faith becomes effective. Each time you communicate your Faith, it brings glory to God.

## Corrupt Communication

*Let no **corrupt communication** proceed out of your mouth, but that which is good to the use of edifying, that it may minister Grace unto the **hearers**. And **grieve not the Holy Spirit** of God* (Ephesians 4:29–30).

I'm not sure why it's so easy and natural for negative words to come out of our mouths. When people get together, the conversation sounds like this: "Did you see what so and so has on?" "I can't believe what so and so said," "Did you hear what he did?" "I don't mean to gossip, but I think you should know . . ." How is any of that beneficial to their spiritual progress? Many have become professionals at gossiping and stick to their profession wherever they go.

The definition of the word *corrupt* in its **Greek form, sapros,** *means rotten, worthless, polluting, and not fitting to the need of the occasion.*

I've been in Bible studies where we studied and discussed a particular topic, and a person would begin to tell a story. After they finished telling their story, people would look around and wonder what in the world it had to do with what we had been talking about. It was corrupt communication that was not fitting for the need of the occasion and had no spiritual benefit for others; it was simply a person enjoying hearing themselves talk.

Corrupt communication does not edify the hearers, pollutes the conversation, is not fitting to the occasion, is worthless, and is not beneficial to the spiritual progress of others. By Faith, we can put a guard over our mouths to stop corrupt communication and become a communicator of every good thing that is in us in Christ Jesus.

*But now I have written unto you **not to keep company**, if any man that is called a brother be a **fornicator,** or **covetous,** or an **idolater**, or a **railer**, or a **drunkard**, or an **extortioner**; with such a one **no not to eat*** (1 Corinthians 5:11).

The Apostle Paul is bold in his warning of the danger of being with those who constantly have corrupt communication. He knows how destructive corrupt communication is to your Faith and warns you not to spend time in fellowship with them. How many times do people, out of obligation, get together in settings where they know no one will talk about the Lord, and the conversation will be nothing but corrupt gossip in the name of "catching up" with what has been going on in their lives? I know you want to use these occasions as a time to be a witness, but how many times have the people you were with said no and rejected the Lord?

The Apostle Paul lists those known for corrupt communication: fornicators, covetous, idolaters, railers, drunkards, and extortioners.

- Fornicators are those who will sell themselves for self-gain.
- Covetous are those who are only thinking of themselves and what they can get from you.
- Idolaters are those who desire to be worshipped.
- Railers are those who are mischievous.
- Drunkards are those who are intoxicated.
- Extortioners are those who take every opportunity to seize control.

What they all have in common is that they're all about themselves and have no interest in you other than what they can take from you. Apostle Paul's wisdom is not to waste your time with those who will steal your Faith with corrupt words. Instead, dust off your feet and take your Faith to those who have not heard the good news.

## Some Will Not Repent

*Lest there be any **fornicator**, or **profane** person, as Esau, who for one morsel of meat **sold his birthright**. For ye know how that afterward, when he would have inherited the **blessing**, **he was rejected**: for he found **no place of repentance**, though he sought it carefully with tears* (Hebrews 12:16–17).

We see here that Esau lived his entire life speaking corrupt communication to satisfy his appetite for self-gain, even to the point of selling his birthright. Even his repentance was corrupt. It was not that he was sorry before God, but he was sorry he missed out on a blessing. He was trying to get a blessing and using a corrupt repentance to get it. God knew his heart was still crooked and rejected his corrupt repentance. Even if Esau had received the blessing, he would have taken it, gone his way, and continued the same lifestyle as before because his heart had not changed.

Many people have come to me and said, *"I know if I talk to my family member one more time, they will repent; I know God is working on them, I know there is a call on their life, and I know . . ."* I have had to ask them lovingly and painfully, *"How many years of one more time have you tried?"* I know you love them, but you need to move on and love the thousands of other people God loves and have not heard even once! Be careful not to get people to "repent" just for the blessing, or they will end up like Esau.

## Recognizing Corrupt Communicators

Have you heard the little jingle, "Oh, be careful little ears what you hear?" This is so important in this day of mass information coming from every direction 24/7. We need to develop an ear to know what Godly communication is and what corrupt communication is. As you listen to things, ask yourself, "Is it beneficial to my spiritual growth or deceptive and self-serving?" As you develop your ear, you may be surprised that corrupt communication will come from unsuspected sources. Many with "good intentions" may not be for your good. Some unlikely sources could be your family, your church family, TV preachers, and those who call themselves Christians. The more you "let the Word become life in your life," the more you will be able to quickly discern corrupt communication when you hear it.

# Simplifying Your Communication

*But **let your communication be, Yea, yea; Nay, nay**: for whatsoever is more than these cometh of evil* (Matthew 5:37).

We are famous for trying to help God by adding a lot of extra flowery speech with elaborate words we feel will make a more remarkable impression. I've heard some who feel the need to preface God's Word with *"The Lord told me; The Lord showed me."* It sounds to me like they are trying to emphasize their own "spirituality" rather than the emphasis being on His Word.

Use the words from the Bible to further simplify your communications. As soon as you start trying to add to the Bible, you could get it all muddled up and corrupted with yourself.

*What thing soever I **command you, observe to do it**: thou shalt **not add thereto, nor diminish from it*** (Deuteronomy 12:32).

God does not want us to make it hard for ourselves. He wants us to say what He says, not add or take away from it. His Word will do the work. He needs us to communicate *His Word*. For example, during one of our live stream services, I had a Word of Knowledge. The Lord uses me in that way often, and someone will always respond with, "That is me." This time I had one word: "cabbage head." Now, I've learned not to add or take away from His Word, so all I said was "cabbage head." The congregation looked around and thought *OK, Bishop has lost his mind.* And to make matters worse, no one responded — not even online. I thought maybe I needed to add a little to this word, like making a cabbage salad, but I just let it go. Two days later, a lady in the church came to me and said that when she got to work the next day, a coworker approached her and said, "That was me, the cabbage head." The coworker said that she was watching online and just checking out our service in her kitchen, watching on her cell phone. When I said cabbage head, she said she was looking at a cabbage head sitting on her counter. She said she immediately burst into tears realizing that God was telling her how much God loves her and knows exactly where she is. Don't add to the Bible, don't add to the gifts of the Spirit, don't add to prophecy. Just say what He says, and God will do only what God can do.

***Every word of God is pure****: he is a shield unto them that put their trust in him.* ***Add thou not unto his words****, lest he reprove thee, and thou be found a liar* (Proverbs 30:5–6).

When God begins to use young ministers in prophecy, they often try to explain what God is saying but misunderstand what He is really speaking to that person. When the prophecy doesn't come to pass, the person will try to make it happen and get into trouble when that's not what God said in the first place. They will scream false prophets, and rightfully so; the minister was lying because of adding something that was not pure and brought dishonor to God.

*For I testify unto every man that heareth the words of the prophecy of this book****, If any man shall add unto these things****, God shall add unto him the plagues that are written in this book:*

*And **if any man shall take away from the words of the book** of this prophecy, God shall take away his part out of the book* *of life, and out of the holy city, and from the things which are written in this book* (Revelation 22:18–19).

This last book in our Bible has intrigued millions over the years desiring to understand the "real" meaning of all the symbolism. More people have probably read more books about this book of Revelation rather than actually reading The Book. Thousands of end-time prophecy teachers have come up with a plethora of explanations of the symbolism and the timing of events. As time passes, old illustrations give way to new ones based on today's technology. I salute all those who have tried to help others understand, and I am in no way knocking their work, as I've taught and written two syllabi on it myself. But in all our gallant attempts to explain this book, it would behoove us to go back to chapter one and verse one.

**The Revelation of Jesus Christ**, *which God gave unto him, to shew unto his servants' things which must shortly come to pass; and he sent and signified it by his angel unto his servant John.* (Revelation 1:1).

You have probably heard, "Keep the main thing the main thing." The main thing this book is about is the revealing of Jesus Christ throughout the book and during the events that are taking place. Have people become more excited and interested in the "other things" and not the main thing, Jesus working in the midst of our tribulations today? The Apostle John wrote to the churches in his day, declaring that Jesus was working in their midst. The good news is that Jesus is working in His church today and will continue to work in the future, no matter what the tribulations His people are going through at the time.

# Correct Bible Interpretation

One sure way of misinterpreting communication is to walk in on the middle of a conversation. Christians are famous for walking in on the middle of a conversation when reading their Bibles. It's easy to search for a scripture, read it out of context, run with it, and try to apply it to your life, but what was the purpose of the scripture to begin with?

If you're going to interpret the Bible correctly, you must go through the questions below. If you don't go through this process, you'll get a half version and misinterpret the purpose of the scripture.

- Who Is Talking? *Moses, an apostle, Jesus, one of the disciples, a heathen*
- Who Is He Talking To? *The Jewish nation, the church, the lost*
- What Is the Message? *Salvation, healing, rebuke, correction, doctrine*
- What Is the Purpose of the Message Being Communicated? *Repentance, Encouragement, Vision*

First and foremost, you must know who is talking. If it's Moses, then we know he's talking to the Jewish nation called out by God to be His representatives on the Earth to take His gospel to the other nations. Moses will be giving God's commandments, laws, statutes, and the heart and instructions from God for the God kind of life.

If it is an apostle, we know they talk mainly to the church, laying doctrine, correction, rebuke, and instruction for evangelism. If it is Apostle Peter, he's talking to the church. If it's Apostle Paul, he's either rebuking the Pharisees, correcting the church, or talking to the lost.

If it's Jesus, He will discuss restoring the covenant between God and man and their relationship with the Heavenly Father. When Jesus speaks to the Pharisees, He will be rebuking them for legalizing the Law of God instead of understanding that the Law of God is our loving Heavenly Father giving us good advice and instructions for a healthy, prosperous, and God kind of life. If Jesus is talking to His disciples, He is training, instructing, and equipping them for the ministry they must continue after His departure. If Jesus is talking to the lost, He will be healing, saving, and demonstrating the love of the Father to the people.

If it's one of the disciples talking, it could range from quoting what Jesus said to sharing their failures, disappointments, and the questions they have in trying to figure out how Faith works. It is not hard to find a disciple we can relate to, as they were going through their training and made numerous mistakes. Seeing how often they failed brings us hope that if we keep going, we will figure it out just like they did.

If it's a heathen talking, you can rest assured that what they're saying is not the Word of God and only a half-truth at best. God tells us to *"learn not the way of the heathen"* (Jeremiah 10:2). If a heathen is talking, he'll be talking about one of his gods who will save them — they range from the sun, moon, planets, fire, wind to gods of fertility and goats, and the list is endless. The heathens have established many festivals to honor their gods, which have morphed into fun celebrations even today, and sadly many Christians unwittingly celebrate them still. Through Moses in the exodus, God brought plagues and judgment to ten of these heathen gods.

One last way we might misunderstand communication in the Bible is by combining two scriptures out of context. This may be a funny and ridiculous example, but it will prove my point. We take the scripture *Judas hanged himself* (Matthew 27:5) and combine it with *go and do likewise* (Luke 10:37). Take the time to ask yourself these four questions: Who is talking, who is he talking to, what is the message, and what is the purpose of the message being communicated, and the Bible will become amazingly clear to you.

## You Shall Be My Witnesses

The four questions will also help you when you want to be a witness to others. Who is talking, who are you talking to, what is your message, and what is the purpose of your message? Are you talking to a Christian, a lost person, a backslidden Christian, or a sick person? Figuring this out will help you determine the message you'll discuss and the purpose you hope to accomplish. You don't have to teach the whole Bible to someone when you witness to them, just a topic that is beneficial to their needs.

# Communication Is Two-Way

Communication involves the following elements:

- Sender
- Message
- Channel
- Receiver

- Response
- Feedback

For communication to be complete, it must be a two-way conversation. If it's not two-way, it's incorrect communication, and you won't know if the message was received correctly. This process may be simple and obvious, but much communication can get lost in translation without it.

Six things must be present to ensure two-way communication:

- A sender for communication to start
- A clear message that needs to be sent
- A channel to send it through, such as voice, email, text, video, or book
- A specific person or group that the message pertains to, as the message does not pertain to everyone
- A response to know whether the message was received
- A time for feedback to clarify that what you said was understood correctly, and without feedback, you'll never know

When I preach, I refuse to be a talking head; I'm always looking for a response, whether a facial expression, an amen, an oh my, a grunt, a groan, a laugh, or applause. I'm always asking questions during my message. Did you get that? Are you still OK? How many are still with me, and did you get anything out of this? I'm not interested in giving a speech but in communication.

It helps to get this feedback. You may be surprised when you ask someone to repeat back what you said. They may say something totally different, so you will need to repeat it, maybe even differently, to help them understand. You will know communication is complete when the feedback reflects the message you intended them to receive.

## Listen Before You Communicate

When we learn something new about Faith, a scripture that came alive, a new revelation, or an answer to prayer, we want to share it with the world. Unfortunately, we start communicating our new message with everyone, oblivious to the needs of the person we're talking to. Maybe we discovered a new revelation about end times and started sharing it with a person who's sick. That person couldn't care less about the future; they're trying to survive the rest of the day. Before we begin our communication, we need to practice the art of listening. For you to know what their need is, you'll have to take time to listen and listen some more because they may not tell you their need upfront. They may be telling you about their symptoms while talking about their day, the past, disappointments, or anger, but you'll have to listen intently to recognize the root problem causing those symptoms. Sometimes you don't need to say anything; just listen. Someone may just want to get something off their chest, and you were the one they dumped it on, but they have no real question for which they want an answer. That's OK. You demonstrated you were someone they could talk to, and they will feel comfortable talking to you again. Don't feel obligated to give an answer to someone who doesn't have a question; wait for another time. Listening to someone demonstrates love. Remember that nobody cares how much you know until they know how much you care.

You will eventually hear the real problem as you learn to listen patiently. As you listen to that person, you'll also be able to listen for God to give you the right word to say that will change their life forever. Learning to be a good listener will make you a great communicator.

## Communication the Lord's Way

*Therefore, speak I to them in parables: because they **seeing see not**; and **hearing they hear not**, neither do they understand* (Matthew 13:13).

Speaking in parables is an excellent way of communicating. Jesus was the walking Word, but He used many parables in His teaching. Parables are realistic illustrations of spiritual truths. It's difficult for many people to read or hear scripture and understand how to apply it in their life. When you take a natural example they understand, you can transition from the natural principle to the spiritual one. Early in my ministry, I was constantly sharing parables about farming, as I was a dairy farmer before entering the ministry. I would talk about planting seeds in my fields for a harvest, then transition to the Word being sown in our hearts and bringing forth a harvest. A great missionary friend told me, "Bill, you're doing a tremendous job on the mission fields because you can speak their language, farming." He went on to tell me he had told some preachers to go back home because their "parables" were about airplanes, and people in the jungle didn't even know what an airplane looked like other than a steak in the sky. We need to learn to talk in the language people are familiar with, such as farmers, youth, businesspeople, lawyers, doctors, factory workers, and whatever their profession is. I will pick one for an example: if you're talking to a lawyer, discuss the legal system and how it operates and then transition into an analogy that God is the judge, the Devil is the prosecuting attorney, Jesus is pleading our case, and the courts of Heaven have set us free according to the Law of God. The possibilities are endless. Open your mind, and you'll find how easy and enjoyable it is to teach in parables and to see the joy when people can see, hear, and understand the Word. They won't argue with the natural principle because they know it's accurate, and they'll find it difficult to argue with the spiritual application.

## God's Word in Our Mouth

We've been learning about the communication of your Faith. Remember that your message should communicate not just your words but the Word of God. Whether you quote scripture, give a parable, give a testimony, or share a teaching, His Word does the work. I will end this chapter with a few scriptures to meditate on as you "let this Word about the communication of your Faith become life in your life."

*If any man speak, let him **speak as the oracles of God**; if any man **minister**, let him do it as of the **ability which God giveth**: that God in all things may **be glorified** through Jesus Christ, to whom be **praise** and dominion for ever and ever. Amen* (1 Peter 4:11).

*But when they shall lead you, and deliver you up, take no thought beforehand what ye shall speak, neither do ye premeditate: but whatsoever shall be given you in that hour, that speak ye: for **it is not ye that speak, but the Holy Ghost*** (Mark 13:11).

*Believest thou not that I am in the Father, and the Father in me?* **The words that I speak unto you I speak not of myself:** *but the Father that dwelleth in me,* **he doeth the works** (John 14:10).

*Now when this was noised abroad, the multitude came together, and were confounded, because that* **every man heard them speak in his own language** (Acts 2:6).

*And* **my speech** *and my preaching was not with enticing words of man's wisdom, but in demonstration of the Spirit and of power: That your Faith should not stand in the wisdom of men, but in the power of God.* **Howbeit we speak wisdom** *among them that are perfect: yet not the wisdom of this world, nor of the princes of this world, that come to nought:* **But we speak the wisdom of God in a mystery**, *even the hidden wisdom, which God ordained before the world unto our glory* (1 Corinthians 2:4–7).

*Withal praying also for us, that God would* **open unto us a door of utterance,** *to* **speak the mystery of Christ**, *for which I am also in bonds: That I may make it manifest,* **as I ought to speak**. *Walk in wisdom toward them that are without,* **redeeming the time. Let your speech be always with Grace,** *seasoned with salt,* **that ye may know how ye ought to answer every man** (Colossians 4:3–6).

## Questions:

- Why is it important to understand proper communication?
- What does it mean that communication becomes effective?

- Have you been a good communicator?
- What defines corrupt communication?
- Have you recognized communicators who are fornicators?
- What is the best way to simplify your communication?
- What is the process for correct Bible interpretation?
- Why should you communicate with parables?
- Has your communication been two-way?
- Is your communication winning souls?

## Prayer Focus:

- Pray that your communication will become effective.
- Pray that your communication brings glory to God.
- Pray that you will not allow corrupt communication to come out of your mouth.
- Pray and repent for any fornication communication of self-exaltation.
- Pray that you learn how to simplify your communication.
- Pray you will apply the Bible interpretation process to your communication.
- Pray that you will make sure your communication is two-way communication.
- Pray that you discern who you are communicating to, the lost or to disciples.
- Pray God will give you parables to effectively talk to the lost.

- Pray that you will make winning souls your main reason for communication.
- Pray that you will periodically evaluate your communication by doing a sound check.
- Pray that you will boldly communicate your Faith now that you understand the process, aspects, and Law of Faith.

# CHAPTER 12

# Faith and the Lord of the Harvest

As we begin this chapter, please read this confession aloud: *"I can have everything the Bible says I can have, I can be everything the Bible says I can be, and I can do everything the Bible says I can do. Today I'm going to let the Word become life in my life."*

## Seed Time Harvest

*While the earth remaineth, seed, time, and harvest, and cold and heat, and summer and winter, and day and night shall not cease* (Genesis 8:22).

God is establishing a law that will remain in effect as long as the Earth remains. Looking outside today, you'll notice the Earth is still here; therefore, this law is still in effect. The winters are still cold, the summers are still hot, and there is still daytime and nighttime. The law of seed, the law of time, and the law of harvest is also still in effect.

If we take this scripture and apply the Three Aspects of Faith, we find The Word of Faith (God said it), The Law of Faith (God is still enforcing it), and The Spirit of Faith (it becomes a lifestyle). We have no problem developing a lifestyle that adapts to living in summer and winter, as we have learned to dress accordingly. Daytime and nighttime determine our work schedules as the clock tells us what to do. What about seed, time, and harvest? Has this principle become a lifestyle?

As with day and night, summer and winter, seed, time, and harvest also go through phases or cycles. There will be a season for seed sowing—the season to plant; a season of time—a waiting period; and finally, a season of harvest—reaping what we have sown. It takes Faith to sow seed, it takes Faith to wait out the time, and it takes Faith to harvest.

It has been said that the seed determines the harvest, but the space of time is very critical regarding the quality and amount of the harvest. I don't know many people with patience as their strong suit as we are a generation of "I want it now!" We must keep our Faith strong during this period to reap our harvest. We can stay strong in Faith, knowing God has determined there will be a season of harvest. My dad used to say, "If it is not in the barn yet, it is not harvested yet." The crop in the field may look beautiful, but it will take Faith to bring it into the barn. When we go to a restaurant, we look at the menu full of seeds we can plant as we place our order, but then there is the space of time when we must wait. What is taking them so long? What are they doing back there? If it's not here in five minutes, I'm leaving. We certainly do not want to have walked out the door the minute they bring the food.

Living in Michigan, I've often heard people say, I sure wish summer would hurry up and get here, and the older I get, I tend to agree with them, but it won't get here before the time. The Law of God will enforce the time, and so it is with the harvest we have sown for.

# Messages from the Harvest

Jesus taught a few parables by comparing his message with what they were familiar with during a harvest season. He knew how best to communicate with those who understood harvests. Others like Jacob and Job saw the Seed Time Harvest principle play out in their lives.

<u>Pray to the Lord of the Harvest</u>

*Then saith he unto his disciples,* **The harvest truly is plenteous**, *but* **the laborers are few;** *Pray ye, therefore,* **the Lord of the harvest**, *that he will send forth laborers into his harvest* (Matthew 9:37–38).

In ancient times, at the start of the harvest, communities would appoint a strong and respected man of the village as their "Lord of the Harvest." He would be responsible for negotiating the harvest wages and organizing the fieldworkers. He would direct the order in which each field should be harvested. He was responsible for ensuring every last sheaf was safely gathered in before declaring the harvest successful and complete.

Jesus beautifully transitions from the natural illustration to the spiritual application of God being the faithful Lord of the Harvest of natural crops and a harvest of souls.

Jesus declared that much seed has been sown, time has expired, and the time of harvest has arrived. The harvest is plenteous, many are ripe and ready to be harvested, and the time has come. Jesus said to His disciples, *Don't say four months, and then comes the harvest; the fields are already white unto harvest* (John 4:35). Jesus explains that the time has come to pray and receive instructions from the Lord of the Harvest and begin to harvest in the fields as He directs.

We often find ourselves "praying for the harvest," expecting God to bring it to us. We don't realize that God has already watched over the harvest through seed and time, and the harvest is right before us in the field. We're still praying for something that's already there. Instead of praying for the harvest, we need to pray to the Lord of the Harvest for His instructions on harvesting it and bringing it in. The harvest is plentiful for those who will go to the field and gather it. Our Faith shifts from Faith in the seed to Faith during time and then to Faith in the Lord of the Harvest.

Jesus has made it clear that the harvest is plenty, and now the Lord of the Harvest is looking for laborers to co-labor with Him in His great harvest of souls. We've been learning the principle of seed, time, and bringing a harvest in many areas of life, including salvation, healing, prosperity, and all the promises of God. God is now looking to you to join Him in His great harvest of souls.

## Laborers Appointed to the Harvest

We see Jesus throughout the gospels demonstrating how to go into the fields and harvest by healing, teaching the Faith, forgiving, delivering, and correcting. Jesus took twelve men with Him to let them see and have training on using the same harvesting techniques He had been doing. Then He appointed them to the harvest and sent them out. *Then he called his twelve disciples together, and gave them power and authority over all devils, and to cure diseases. And he sent them to preach the kingdom of God, and to heal the sick. And he said unto them, Take nothing for your journey, neither staves, nor scrip, neither bread, neither money; neither have two coats apiece. And whatsoever house ye enter into, there abide, and thence depart. And whosoever will not receive you, when ye go out of that city, shake off the very dust from your feet for a testimony against them. And they departed, and went through the towns, preaching the gospel, and healing everywhere* (Luke 9:1–6).

Jesus reminded the disciples of the principle of the Lord of the Harvest that he would take care of their wages and needs as he sends them into the harvest. Jesus then took on the Lord of the Harvest role and appointed another seventy that He sent into the harvest.

*After these things,* **the Lord appointed other seventy** *also and sent them two and two before his face into every city and place, whither* **he himself would come**. *Therefore, said he unto them,* **The harvest truly is great**, *but the* **laborers are few***: pray ye, therefore,* **the Lord of the harvest***, that he would* **send forth laborers into his harvest** (Luke 10:1–2).

The Lord of the Harvest is still looking to appoint more laborers into His great harvest of today. Throughout the ages, there has never been a problem with seed, time, and harvest, but there has always been a problem with not having enough laborers. Many simply do not want to work; others have not had the training to be effective, while others did not even know that God would wish to allow them to be a part of such a great work. Join me in praying to the Lord of the Harvest that He would send laborers into the harvest and let one of them be me.

The prophet Joel describes many different dynamics happening during harvest: a natural yield of crops, time of gathering, time of judgment, time of war, the Day of the Lord, and multitudes in a time of decision.

*Beat your **plowshares into swords** and your **pruning-hooks into spears**: let the weak say, I am strong. **Assemble yourselves**, and come, all ye heathen, and gather yourselves together round about: thither cause thy mighty ones to come down, O LORD. Let the heathen be wakened and come up to the valley of Jehoshaphat: for there **will I sit to judge** all the heathen roundabout. **Put ye in the sickle, for the harvest is ripe**: come, get you down; for the press is full, the fats overflow; for their wickedness is great. **Multitudes, multitudes in the valley of decision:** for **the day of the LORD is near in the valley of decision*** (Joel 3:10–14).

We must determine our season. Do I need plow shears or a sword to fight before planting? Do I need a pruning hook to cut off the excess or a spear to drive off the enemy? Am I being judged, and do I need to warn others of the coming judgment? During harvest time, something or someone is always trying to steal your harvest. Bugs, birds, animals, weather, storms, wind, hail, or people will destroy natural crops. In the spiritual crop, they can be people, demons, unbelief, doubt, and a lack of Faith.

Multitudes are in the Valley of Decisions every day. Daily and even hourly, we need to make decisions. We decide to go or stay, buy or not, say yes or no, eat this or not, agree or disagree, and the list of decisions continues throughout our day. We must be aware that a war is going on in our minds whenever we face a decision. Our decision determines the harvest, whether it will be a good or bad harvest.

When you share the Word of God with someone, a spiritual war begins in their mind. Demons get involved and endeavor to influence the person to say no to the Word; a "not yet" or "maybe later" is still a no. When the Word of God comes to you, I encourage you to use your harvesting tools and the weapons of warfare to bring in your harvest of the promises of God.

The Day of the Lord comes when the heathen, the mighty ones, kings, and rulers gather against God in the final Valley of Decision. On this day, God will make the final decision based upon their decision to reject and come against Him. God has been long-suffering, but He must decide to cut off and crush the revolt as grapes in a great winepress of judgment. In other scriptures, this is referred to as a day of destruction, darkness, division, and the battle of Armageddon, at which time God will cast out Satan and all his hosts, and then there will be a time of peace on the Earth for one thousand years.

## Jacob's Ladder

There is a story in Genesis about Jacob's ladder dream that most Christians are familiar with but never considered it was about the Lord of the Harvest.

*And he **dreamed**, and **behold a ladder** set up on the earth, and the **top of it reached to Heaven**: and behold the **angels of God ascending and descending on it**. And behold, the LORD stood above it, and said, I am the LORD God of Abraham thy* *father, and the God of Isaac: the land whereon thou liest, to thee will **I give it, and to thy seed*** (Genesis 28:12–13).

The Lord will often speak to us in dreams to give us a visual of something supernatural that's happening that we're not aware of. The ladder reaches Heaven where the Lord of the Harvest is sitting. The Lord of the Harvest watches over the seed sown in each generation, the seed that Abraham planted in the land, the seed that Isaac sowed in the ground, and the land that Jacob is now in. The Lord is showing Jacob he is now going to inherit the harvest of the seeds sown over the years from the previous generations. If Jacob continues sowing, the Lord of the Harvest will guarantee a harvest for the next generation. We see here the principle of seed, time, and harvest that continues throughout each generation. Jacob's name was later changed to Israel, from which came the twelve tribes of Israel. The Lord of the Harvest declared that He would give the land to his seed, and we have the land of Israel today.

Jacob's ladder dream about the Lord of the Harvest also relates to us today. *There is neither Jew nor Greek, there is neither bond nor free, there is neither male nor female: for ye are all one in Christ Jesus. And **if ye be Christ's, then are ye Abraham's seed**, and **heirs according to the promise*** (Galatians 3:28–29). We can also receive the blessing by applying the Three Aspects of Faith and the principle of seed, time, and harvest. *That **the blessing of Abraham might come on the Gentiles through Jesus Christ**; that **we might receive the promise of the Spirit through faith*** (Galatians 3:14).

An essential part of Jacob's dream is that angles ascend and descend to and from the Lord of the Harvest. The word *angel* is translated from the Hebrew word—***malak***—*messenger, prophet, priest, ambassador, angel.* Without understanding the Hebrew word for angels, we immediately think it only talks about God's supernatural angels. Still, this word can also include a prophet or priest. *God has made us priests and kings unto our God* (Revelation 5:10). As priests in the Kingdom, we can go to the Lord of the Harvest and come boldly to the throne (Hebrews 4:16). Many Christians have not received their harvest because they have not known they could approach the Lord of the Harvest and boldly come to His throne to claim the harvest that was legally and rightfully theirs.

A crop farmer in my area had hundreds of acres that he owned or rented and planted many crops. A nearby farmer asked him why he had not harvested a crop next to him; the farmer replied, "I forgot I even had that field!" I wonder how often we have forgotten the seeds we have sown or grown weary in waiting and missed our harvest. I encourage you to climb the ladder in prayer today and ask the Lord of the Harvest to release what you've been sowing and believing for. You can claim the harvest from the seed you've sown; it is The Law of Faith.

Satan and his angels are also interested in the harvest and are ascending and descending this ladder. They know this principle. They don't miss a beat, and every time there's time for a harvest, they're up that ladder. Satan is a legalist and knows that people will receive according to their seed, whether they sowed good seed or bad seed. Satan wants to ensure the Lord of the Harvest will bring the harvest from the bad seed and try to accuse and make a legal case of why they should not receive from the good seed (Revelation 12:10). We must ensure that we're sowing the good seed of the Word of God and pray for "crop failure" from the bad seed we've sown by asking for forgiveness.

When Jacob awoke from his sleep, he immediately understood the supernatural things happening daily. I wonder how many of us are asleep spiritually and unaware of the Lord of the Harvest principle preventing us from receiving our harvest.

*And **Jacob awaked out of his sleep**, and he said, Surely **the LORD is in this place; and I knew it not**. And he was afraid, and said, **How dreadful is this place!** This is none other but the house of God, and this is **the gate of heaven** (Genesis 28:16–17).*

The word *sleep* is translated from the Hebrew word **shekah,** which means slackness. In a previous chapter, we found that slackness was one of the enemies of God that stole our harvest. When we are slacking in operating in the principle of the Lord of the Harvest, we will miss out on many blessings that the Lord has intended for us to have. It is time to "wake up" to what happens daily in our harvest field.

Jacob was afraid and said this was a dreadful place to be in; he was unaware that the Lord of the Harvest was watching over the seed he had sown and was about to give him his harvest. Why was Jacob afraid and not joyful? He was optimistic about the land's harvest but also realized he was about to harvest from the bad seed he had sown. He realized he received a harvest from his dealings with his brother Esau. He experienced that harvest with Laban, who deceived him as he did Esau. Remember, *Be not deceived; God is not mocked: for whatsoever a man soweth, that shall he also reap* (Galatians 6:7). When we say, "Where'd that come from," well, it came from what you sowed. The Lord of the Harvest is very legal, and Satan is also a legalist; you will not have a harvest you did not sow for.

## Job's Continual Sowing

*And it was so, when the days of their feasting were gone about, that Job sent and sanctified them, and rose up early in the morning, and **offered burnt offerings** according to the number of them all: for Job said, **It may be** that my sons have sinned, and cursed God in their hearts. **Thus did Job continually*** (Job 1:5).

Job's sons always had all sorts of parties, and you know what can happen at parties. Parents get concerned when their teens go to parties because they remember all too well what they used to do at parties when they were young.

*Now there was a day when the **sons of God** came to present themselves before the LORD, and **Satan came also among them**. And the LORD said unto Satan, Whence comest thou? Then Satan answered the LORD, and said, From going to and fro in the earth, and from walking up and down in it* (Job 1:6–7).

When it is time for your harvest, Satan will be right there with you. The Lord asked Satan where he came from, and Satan answered from going to and fro in the earth, where he watched the seed sown. Why did God ask Satan? Because God knew if Satan was there, he had a legal right to a harvest that he wanted the Lord of the Harvest to hand out legally. Satan is there to bring the harvest that Job had sown through fear.

Job continued sowing and offering sacrifices out of fear for what his sons may or may not have done. Job sowed thoughts of fear and sacrificed to fear, and he did this continually. I've often said that an acronym for fear is **f**alse **e**vidence **a**ppearing **r**eal; whether he confirmed that his sons sinned or not, false evidence was real to him. Satan hated that God had blessed Job, and he finally found a legal right to get back at Job by using the seed he sowed to fear. The seed starts with thoughts, moves into words, then into action, and finally comes the harvest. We must guard ourselves with this scripture, *Casting down imaginations, and every high thing that exalteth itself against the knowledge of God and bringing into captivity every thought to the obedience of Christ* (2 Corinthians 10:5).

Job eventually realizes he cannot blame God for what has come to him; his fear and sowing brought this harvest.

*For* **the thing which I greatly feared is come upon me, and that which I was afraid of is come unto me** (Job 3:25).

Fear is one of the greatest tools that Satan uses against us. Fear works like Faith but only to the negative. Fear is simply believing in something, whether we realize it or not. Jesus said many times in scripture, "Fear not!" Satan cannot bring a harvest you have not sown for. Many chapters in the book of Job tell how Job is trying to explain this principle to his friends, but they offer their own "spiritual" ideas, which all are wrong. Job is simply trying to explain that he cannot blame God or even Satan; his own sowing to fear caused it. The good news is that once Job understood the Lord of the Harvest principle, he got rid of fear and started sowing in Faith, and his harvest, in the end, was twice what he had before. *And the LORD turned the captivity of Job when he* *prayed for his friends: also **the LORD gave Job twice as much as he had before*** (Job 42:10).

God has established the right to climb this ladder and legally claim your harvest. Decide today that you will not sow fear anymore, and if you do, ask for a "crop failure" by asking for forgiveness. Sow the Word of God in Faith and come joyfully to the Lord of the Harvest.

# Whatever We Sow

*Be not deceived; God is not mocked: for **whatsoever a man soweth, that shall he also reap.** For he that **soweth to his flesh** shall of the flesh **reap corruption**, but he that **soweth to the Spirit** shall of the Spirit **reap life everlasting**. And let us not be weary in well doing: for **in due season we shall reap**, if we faint not* (Galatians 6:7–9).

Do not be deceived about the Lord of the Harvest principle. Whatever you have sown is precisely what you will reap. God established the law of seed, time, and harvest in the beginning, and is still operating today. The Lord of the Harvest watches over the harvest and will not allow any illegal harvest to occur. We won't be able to trick God into a harvest we did not sow for, and the enemy can't give us a harvest we did not sow for. God has entrusted us with the authority to sow and reap whatever we desire. We may get a quick crop if we sow to the flesh, but it will not be what we want in the end. It may take a little longer to sow to the spirit, but if we don't weary in well doing in due season, we shall reap, and it will be what we want. If we sow to the flesh, it may be quick, easy, and satisfying but temporary. If we sow to the spirit, it may take some time, energy, Faith, and endurance, but it will be everlasting.

## White Already to Harvest

***Jesus saith unto them, My meat is to do the will of him that sent me, and to finish his work.***

***Say not ye, There are yet four months, and then cometh harvest?*** *behold, I say unto you, Lift up your eyes, and look on the fields; for they are* ***white already to harvest***. *And* ***he that reapeth receiveth wages***, *and* ***gathereth fruit*** *unto life eternal: that both he that soweth and he that reapeth may rejoice together* (John 4:34–36).

Jesus chose twelve disciples and taught them all things pertaining to the Kingdom of God. He taught them and demonstrated before them:

- The Three Aspects of Faith
- How the Just Shall Live by Faith
- The Five Levels of Faith
- The Blessings of Faith
- The Process of Faith
- The Law of Faith
- How to Keep the Faith
- How the Holy Spirit Works in The Five Levels of Faith
- How Demons Work in the Three Aspects of Faith
- How Faith Scatters the Enemies
- How to Communicate Their Faith
- Faith and The Lord of The Harvest.

Jesus then challenges His disciples to look and see that the fields are ready for harvest, not to wait, and to be about the Father's business. Jesus assures them that the Lord of the Harvest will reward them for their work in the harvest fields. The Father has great joy when His children walk in Faith and receive His blessings, and now He will have His greatest enjoyment when His children work with Him in bringing lost souls into His eternal Kingdom.

After learning these same principles throughout the chapters, I sincerely ask that you join with the Father in His harvest fields. You now have the same tools of Faith that Jesus used so you can do it also. Remember what Jesus said in John 5:19 and John 14:10–12:

*Then answered Jesus and said unto them, Verily, verily, I say unto you,* **The Son can do nothing of himself,** *but what he seeth the Father do: for what things soever he doeth, these also doeth the Son likewise* (John 5:19).

You can do nothing in and of yourself, but if you can see what the Father is doing, you can do it also.

*Believest thou not that I am in the Father, and the Father in me? The words that I speak unto you I speak not of myself: but* **the Father that dwelleth in me, he doeth the works.** *Believe me that I am in the Father, and the Father in me: or else believe me for the very works' sake. Verily, verily, I say unto you,* **He that believeth on me, the works that I do shall he do also;** *and greater works than these shall he do; because I go unto my Father* (John 14:10–12).

Do you believe you are in the Father, and the Father, through His Word and Spirit, is in you? If you believe this, the Father will work through you as you walk in a lifestyle of Faith. "Let the Word become life in your life!"

*And **sow the fields**, and **plant vineyards**, which may yield fruits of increase* (Psalm 107:37).

There are many different fields and vineyards to sow in: youth, schools, families, marriages, divorced people, single parents, addicts, homeless people, businesses, and everywhere people are. What field tugs at your heartstrings that you can see the Father desiring to work in? As you step out in Faith and go forth, the Father will work with you, confirming His Word with signs following (Luke 16:20).

***They that sow in tears shall reap in joy.*** *He that goeth forth and weepeth, bearing precious seed, shall doubtless come again with rejoicing, **bringing his sheaves with him*** (Psalms 126:5).

It's time for the church again to move out into the hurting world with compassion, weeping for the lost and bearing precious seeds of the Word of the Kingdom. As we labor with the Lord of the Harvest, we sing an old hymn, "We shall come rejoicing, bringing in the sheaves."

## Understanding the Kingdom of God

Jesus often taught in parables to help us understand the principles of the Kingdom of God. Parables use a realistic illustration of what people are familiar with and then transition into a spiritual comparison revealing how the Kingdom of God operates. In several of these parables, Jesus uses the law of seed, time, and harvest. Jesus tells a parable in Matthew

13:1–9 about how sowing seeds in different kinds of ground, the process of time, and the quantity of harvest expected. He transitions from the natural illustration to the spiritual application in the following verses.

*When anyone heareth the word of the kingdom, and* **understandeth it not**, *then cometh the wicked one, and catcheth away that which was sown in his heart. This is he which received seed by the wayside. But he that received the seed into stony places, the same is he that heareth the word, and anon with joy receiveth it; Yet hath he, not root in himself, but dureth for a while: for when tribulation or persecution ariseth because of the word, by and by he is offended. He also that received seed among the thorns is he that heareth the word; and the care of this world, and the deceitfulness of riches, choke the word, and he becometh unfruitful. But he that received seed into the good ground is he that heareth the word, and* **understandeth it**, *which also beareth fruit, and bringeth forth, some a hundredfold, some sixty, some thirty* (Matthew 13:19–23).

Jesus explains why it's imperative to hear the Word of the Kingdom and understand the principle of the law of seed, time, and harvest. When the wicked one sees that we do not understand the principles of the Kingdom, he knows he can immediately steal the Word that could have produced our harvest. Have you considered the Kingdom of God is all about seed, time, and harvest? God's plan is for this law to work for you and bring forth a 30, 60, and 100-fold harvest! The Lord of the Harvest is watching over the seed and the type of ground the seed is sown in and will bring forth the best harvest possible.

The enemies of God are also watching over the seed, trying to steal the seed, and using five specific ways to affect the ground, which choke out the harvest. Jesus systematically describes what the enemy uses to steal the Word, our joy and strength, and distracts us from using our Faith to bring in our harvest:

- **Affliction** — pressure, burden, trouble, tribulation
- **Persecution** — mistreated because of religious belief
- **Cares of this world** — distractions, divide, give self to, consumed with
- **Deceitfulness of riches** — delusion, apathy, false hope, or belief
- **Lusts of other things** — desires, longing, covet, set focus on

The enemy uses each of these to wear us down, cause us to grow weary, and drain our strength until we're too tired to work our Faith for the harvest. I preached a message called "Tired of Being Tired?" I addressed why many people ask, "Why am I so tired all the time?" Everybody seems tired all day, young and old, Christian and sinner, and if they don't say it out loud, they act like it. The definition of *tired* is drained of strength, low on energy, exhausted, spent, stale, and bored.

The causes can vary from physical, mental, and spiritual issues. Physical causes can come from anemia, diabetes, thyroid, heart disease, nutritional deficiencies, sleep apnea, menopause, and being overweight. The good news is ***With His stripes you are healed*** (1 Peter 2:24). Mental causes can come from mental fatigue, weariness, irritability, lethargy, depression, anxiety, prolonged stress, demanding jobs, procrastination, tragic events, grief, anger, and loneliness. The good news is ***Thou wilt keep him in perfect peace, whose mind is stayed on thee****: because he trusteth in thee* (Isaiah 26:3). The spiritual causes come from affliction, persecution, cares of this life, the deceitfulness of riches, and the lust for other things. The good news is found in the parable that Jesus so eloquently presented, describing the Word of the Kingdom and the principle of seed, time, and harvest.

Once we understand how the Kingdom of God operates, we are assured that God desires His Word to produce a complete harvest in our lives. We will recognize what the enemy uses to steal our harvest and begin to take care of our ground by sowing, watering, cultivating, weeding, and chasing away the enemy by Faith. We need to be responsible, "response-able," not just busy doing but having the ability to respond correctly with the Word of God. When we realize the enemy is simply trying to steal our strength and joy, we will respond like Nehemiah, ***"The Joy of the Lord is your strength"*** (Nehemiah 8:10). Jesus set the example of overcoming by joy, *Looking unto Jesus the author and finisher of our faith; who **for the joy that was set before him endured the cross*** (Hebrews 12:2). Focus on the joy of harvest, and you will get through all the battles. Don't let the enemy steal your joy but increase in joy (Isaiah 29:19), be full of joy (Psalm 16:11), and obtain everlasting joy (Isaiah 51:11).

## More Parables to Explain the Kingdom of God

*Another parable put he forth unto them, saying,* ***The kingdom of Heaven is like*** *to a grain of mustard* ***seed****, which* ***a man took****, and* ***sowed*** *in his field: Which indeed is the* ***least of all seeds****: but when* ***it is grown****, it is the greatest among herbs,* *and becometh a tree, so that **the birds of the air come and lodge in the branches thereof*** (Matthew 13:31–32).

In this parable, Jesus describes how small and insignificant a seed can seem but still have significant power to become a great tree. Have you ever been amazed at how God put a beautiful oak tree with all the leaves and colors inside a little acorn? How about a beautiful evergreen tree that stays green all through the winter inside a little pine cone? One little Word from God, whether from a book or a sermon, can produce an amazing life-changing transformation for the rest of your life. Again, Jesus reminds us that the enemy knows the seed's power to transform you and tries to steal your fruit, so don't let them build a nest in your life.

*And he said unto them, **Take heed what ye hear**: with **what measure ye mete**, it shall be measured to you: and unto you that hear shall more be given. For he that hath, to him shall be given: and he that hath not, from him shall be taken even that which he hath. And he said, So is **the Kingdom of God, as if a man should cast seed into the ground**; And should sleep, and rise night and day, and the seed should spring and grow up, he knoweth not how. For the earth bringeth forth fruit of herself; first the blade, then the ear, after that the full corn in the ear. But when the fruit is brought forth, immediately he putteth in the sickle, because the harvest is come* (Mark 4:24–29).

In this parable, Jesus warns us about how spiritual seed is sown and says to heed what you hear. The enemy knows the power of words and how they're seeds that produce after their kind. Oh, be careful, little ears, what you hear! In the beginning, God created the seed principle and said it was good (Genesis 1:11–12). The man and woman were not in the garden very long before the enemy started sowing words into them by sowing doubt and good and evil seeds (Genesis 3:1–5). We may not recognize the tiny seed that's sown, but as time goes on, the seed begins to spring up, first the blade, then the ear, and after that, the complete harvest. The harvest will reveal the kind of seed that was sown. God's plan is for His Word to be planted in our lives. It may take some time, but we can stay in Faith, knowing it will produce a great harvest in our lives. Jesus continues and explains the amount of yield compared to the amount of seed we mete out or sow. Determine that you will hear and speak the Word continually and eventually start harvesting every day. You can't get too much Word into your life and do not have to fear an overdose.

## When to Use Parables

*And **with many such parables spake he the word unto them**, as they were able to hear it. But **without a parable spake he not unto them**: and **when they were alone, he expounded all things to his disciples*** (Mark 4:33–34).

When Jesus was speaking to the lost, He always used parables as a natural illustration to explain a spiritual truth. When He was alone with His disciples, He explained the parables more in-depth, as they could hear and understand the principles of the Kingdom of God. As ministers, we need to learn what people are able to hear and understand. When I first started pastoring a church, I thought if they walked through the door, they all wanted to hear the deep things of God. I soon learned that some needed an encouraging word, a hug, a smile, a God loves you, or a simple prayer. I realized I had to save the deeper truths for those who attended my Bible school and were able to hear them. When Jesus talked with the lost, He used parables; when He spoke with the sick, He healed them; and when He talked to His disciples, He taught, corrected, and disciplined them. Jesus gave milk to the babies in Christ and meat to the disciples, and both are the love of God.

## Parables Teaching That Temptation Will Come but Not from God

*My brethren, count it all joy when ye fall into* **diverse temptations***, Knowing this, that the trying of your faith worketh patience. But let patience have her perfect work, that ye may be perfect and entire, wanting nothing* (James 1:2–4).

The Apostle James is writing to the church, and therefore he is speaking a more in-depth teaching that seems to be a little hard to swallow. After all, why would I possibly be joyful about temptations and trials? If we read this in Greek, it's easier to understand. *My fellow disciples consider with gladness and calm delight when you fall into or are surrounded by and encounter different adversities that will try your faith. Know this that when your faith is put to the test you will perceive that your faith will not only stand but become stronger and more consistent.* That sounds better; temptation is not as bad as I thought. Faith that is not proven is not trustworthy. When I was in my high school welding class, my teacher would make me take my weld, put it in a vice, take a hammer, and bend it entirely over to see if it would break. If it broke, my weld was not trustworthy, but if it stood the beating, I counted it all joy. Later in life, when I had to weld machinery on the farm, I was confident that my welds would stand the pressure. The same with the test of our Faith; when our Faith stands the test, we can be sure our Faith is perfect and won't want, fail, or lack anything when other more difficult tests come our way.

***Blessed is the man that endureth temptation****: for when he is tried, he shall receive the crown of life, which the Lord hath promised to them that love him.* ***Let no man say when he is tempted, I am tempted of God: for God cannot be tempted with evil, neither tempteth he any man: But every man is tempted, when he is drawn away of his own lust, and enticed****. Then when lust hath **conceived**, it **bringeth forth** sin: and sin, when it is **finished**, bringeth forth death.* ***Do not err, my beloved brethren Every good gift*** *and every perfect gift is from above, and cometh down from the Father of lights, with whom is no variableness, neither shadow of turning* (James 1:12–17).

When we endure and remain strong in Faith during a test or trial, we find ourselves blessed and in a position to receive from God what He has promised: victory, crown, and prize. James clarifies that God cannot tempt any man with evil because every good and perfect gift comes from God. James explains that everyone will be tempted and makes sure we know where and how temptation comes. Temptation comes from our lust or desire to be lazy and take shortcuts. Just like in my welding example, if I had gotten lazy and hurried to get my piece done to get out of class early, it would have broken, and I would have had to weld it again. If we get lazy with our Faith and do not take the time to go through the Three Aspects of Faith, the test will break our Faith, and we'll have to start over. Refuse the temptation to hurry your Faith and enjoy the journey.

When I was homeschooling my son in a math class, he was tired of solving all the problems on the page. He finally finished and was pretty happy, but then he turned the page and found more problems to solve. He looked up at me and said, "This book is nothing but problems." Life is and will always be full of problems! We'll never live in a bubble without difficulties, tests, trials, and temptations, but we can count it all joy knowing that the trying of our Faith will work consistently in our life, and we will want for nothing.

*But **be ye doers of the word, and not hearers only**, deceiving your own selves. For if any be **a hearer of the word, and not a doer**, he is like unto a man beholding his natural face in a glass: For he beholdeth himself, and goeth his way, and straightway **forgetteth** what manner of man he was. But whoso looketh into the perfect law of liberty, and continueth therein, he being not a forgetful hearer, but **a doer of the work, this man shall be blessed in his deed**. If any man among you seem to be religious, and **bridleth not his tongue**, but deceiveth his own heart, this man's religion is vain* (James 1:22–26).

Have you ever stood up and walked into another room, and when you got there, you thought what in the world did I come out here for? Maybe you needed something from the store, and when you got there, you started looking around, picked up a few things, and went back home, then you realized you forgot the main thing you went to the store for in the first place. My wife and I travel a lot of miles for meetings, and we will be driving along and enjoying our conversation. Suddenly, I realize I'm not sure where I am. Did I miss my exit? The Apostle James tells us we must hear the Word and pay attention to our actions. Are we still doing the word, or did we forget and get distracted with something else? It's easy to do. We need to bridle our tongues and ensure we're still speaking the Word concerning the blessing and harvest we set out to get.

## By Faith, Begin to Praise God for Our Harvest

*Let the people praise thee, O God; let all the people praise thee.* ***Then shall the earth yield her increase****, and God, even our own God, shall bless us. God shall bless us, and all the ends of the earth shall fear him* (Psalms 67:5–7).

Let the Word become life in your life.

## Questions:

- Why is it essential to understand seed time harvest?
- Why are there few laborers in the harvest?
- Why is it important to discern the seasons of harvest?
- Why was Jacob fearful of the Lord of the Harvest?
- Why did Job receive a "bad" harvest?
- What were the Kingdom of God parables mainly about?
- Why should we be aware of what we sow too?
- Have you considered your city as a field and vineyard?
- How many seeds do you need to sow to receive your desired harvest?
- Can you see yourself rejoicing, bringing in the sheaves?

## Prayer Focus:

- Pray that you will better understand seed, time, and harvest principles.
- Pray that you will become an active laborer in the harvest.
- Pray that you will discern the harvest seasons, planting time, and harvest time.
- Pray that you will be mindful of the seed you are sowing so you won't be fearful in harvest time.
- Pray that you will never sow into fear.
- Pray for understanding the parables from a seed, time, and harvest perspective.
- Pray that you will always be aware of what and to what you are sowing into.
- Pray that you will see your city as a field and vineyard that you can sow into.
- Pray that your sowing time will increase daily.
- Pray you will not leave any harvest in the field through missed opportunities.
- Pray to the Lord of the Harvest that He will send more laborers into the harvest.
- Pray that you will see yourself "Rejoicing Bringing in the Sheaves."
- Pray that you will "let the Word become life in your life."

# CHAPTER 13
# Life After Death

As we begin this chapter, please read this confession aloud: *"I can have everything the Bible says I can have, I can be everything the Bible says I can be, and I can do everything the Bible says I can do. Today I'm going to let the Word become life in my life."*

People have asked, "Is there life after death" throughout the centuries? As we begin to find out what the Bible says about life after death, we need to consider a few other questions:

- What is life?
- What is death?
- Is there life before death?
- What kind of life is before death?
- What kind of life is after death?

## What Is Life?

Approximately 549 verses use the word *life* in the Bible. I certainly will not share all of those with you today, but we can understand more clearly by looking at the Hebrew and

Greek words from which the word life is translated. The two Hebrew words are *chay* and *nephesh,* and the two Greek words are *psuche* and *zoe.* Every time you see the word *life* in the Bible, the meaning comes from one of these four words.

The Hebrew word *chay* means alive or living. This includes every living creature, whether animal, plant, fish, or bird. *And God said, Let the waters bring forth abundantly the moving creature that hath **life** and fowl that may fly above the earth in the open firmament of heaven. And God created great whales, and every **living** creature that moveth, which the waters brought forth abundantly, after their kind, and every winged fowl after his kind: and God saw that it was good. And God blessed them, saying, Be fruitful, and multiply, and fill the waters in the seas, and let fowl multiply in the earth* (Genesis 1:20–22).

The Hebrew word *nephesh* means breathing creature, appetite, desire, and mortal existence liable to die, including man and animals capable of having desires and appetites. *And to every beast of the earth, and to every fowl of the air, and to everything that creepeth upon the earth, wherein there is **life**, I have given every green herb for meat: and it was so* (Genesis 1:28–30).

The Greek word *psuche* means breath, spirit, soul, mind, will, and emotions. *Psuche* is specific to man, demons, and angels whom God has given the ability to decide their actions by their own will. *For whosoever will save **his life** shall lose it; but whosoever shall lose his life for my sake and the gospel's, the same shall save it. For what shall it profit a man if he shall gain the whole world and lose his own soul?* (Mark 8:35–36).

The Greek word *zoe* means quick, alive, to live, to have the God kind of life compared to the natural life without the God in their life. *Enter ye in at the strait gate: for wide is the gate, and broad is the way, that leadeth to destruction, and many there be which go in thereat: Because strait is the gate, and narrow is the way,* **which leadeth unto life***, and few there be that find it* (Matthew 7:13–14).

Every time we see the word *life* in scripture, it talks about a different kind of life. God has created life, and we see it all around us in plants, trees, animals, fish, humankind, and the spirit world. Life is a precious gift from God, and He has purposed for us to have life and have it more abundantly. *The thief cometh not, but for to steal, and to kill, and to destroy: I am come that they might have* **life** *and that they might* **have it more abundantly** (John 10:10).

## What Is Death?

Approximately 456 verses use the word *death* in the Bible. I certainly will not share all those with you today, but we can understand more clearly by looking at the Hebrew and Greek words from which death is translated.

The three Hebrew words are *maveth, ratsach, and tsalmaveth,* and the three Greek words are *teleute, thanatos, and epithanatios.* Every time you see the word *death* in the Bible, the meaning comes from one of these six words.

The Hebrew word *maveth* means natural death, ruin, destroy, the place or state of the dead. *And he said, Behold now, I am old, I know not the day of my death* (Genesis 27:2).

The Hebrew word *ratsach* means to kill, slay, or murder, a death sentence. *Whoso killeth any person, the murderer shall be put to death by the mouth of witnesses: but one witness shall not testify against any person to cause him to die. Moreover, ye shall take no satisfaction for the life of a murderer, which is guilty of death: but he shall be surely put to death* (Numbers 35:30–31).

The Hebrew word *tsalmaveth* means the grave, the shadow of death. *Before I go, whence I shall not return, even to the land of darkness and the shadow of death. A land of darkness, as darkness itself; and of the shadow of death, without any order, and where the light is as darkness* (Job 10:21–22).

The Greek word *teleute* means decease, deceased, to finish, to expire, to die. *And was there until the death of Herod: that it might be fulfilled which was spoken of the Lord by the prophet, saying, Out of Egypt have I called my son* (Matthew 2:15).

The Greek word *thanatos* means deadly, to crush, or darkness. *The people which sat in darkness saw great light, and to them which sat in the region and shadow of death light is sprung up* (Matthew 4:16). *Verily I say unto you, There be some standing here, which shall not taste of death, till they see the Son of man coming in his kingdom* (Matthew 16:28).

The Greek word *epithanatios* means doomed to death, appointed to death. *For I think that God hath set forth us the apostles last, as it were **appointed to death**: for we are made a spectacle unto the world, and to angels, and to men* (1 Corinthians 4:9). *And as it is appointed unto men once to die, but after this the judgment* (Hebrews 9:27).

I have heard it said that there are two absolutes in life: death and taxes. Death has an appointment on our calendars; we may not know the exact date, but it will come. The good news is that we will soon discover that "life after death" exists!

## Is There Life Before and After Death?

We are living and breathing, have appetites and desires, have a rational soul, and are mortal, so it is obvious that we have a life now, whether that is *chay, nephesh, or psuche*. Many say, "There must be more to life than this!" The good news is that there *is* more to life, called *zoe*. We have the opportunity for the God kind of life now.

The Sadducees believed in the Torah and taught that we could have a good life if we followed God's instructions. If we did not follow God's Torah, we would receive judgment in this life. But after that, the soul went into blackness and nothingness. That is why they are Sad-You-See.

*All the commandments which I command thee this day shall ye observe to do,* **that ye may live** *(chay), and multiply, and go in and possess the land which the LORD sware unto your fathers* (Deuteronomy 8:1). *Keep my commandments, and live (chay), and my law as the apple of thine eye* (Proverbs 7:2).

The Pharisees believed not only in the Torah for a good life now but also in the prophets and the writings that promised the resurrection and immortality. Many believe in their "best life now," but there is so much more, as we will see.

## What Kind of Life Is Before Death?

The kind of life we live before death is simply that we are alive and breathing, have appetites and desires, are mortal, and have rational souls. We also have the opportunity for the God kind of life obtained by following the Torah, Prophets, the Writings, and trusting Jesus.

## Is There Life After Death?

Yes, there is. The kind of life we live after death is the God kind of life and is eternal. We are awakened from sleep and inactivity to experience God's purpose and future for our lives as we collect our faculties and come to our senses.

There are approximately 100 verses using words about life after death in the Bible. I certainly am not going to share all of those with you today, but we can gain a clear understanding by looking at the Greek words from which the phrase "eternal life" is translated.

The Greek word *anastasis* means resurrection, a rising from the dead. *Jesus said unto her, I am the* **resurrection** *(anastasis), and the* **life** *(zoe): he that believeth in me, though he were dead, yet shall he live* (John 11:25). Jesus tells Martha that He has the power of life after death and the God kind of life now that He is about to give to Lazarus.

The Greek word *aionios* means eternal, perpetual, forever, everlasting, never to cease, and future. *For God so loved the world, that he gave his only begotten Son, that whosoever believeth in him should not perish, but have* **everlasting** *(aionios)* **life** *(zoe)* (John 3:16). This verse is probably the most famous in the Bible to many; however, without seeing the Greek words, we miss a powerful truth. If we believe, trust, cling to, and rely on Jesus, we can have the God kind of life (*zoe*) now and **everlasting** *(aionios)* life for eternity.

The Greek word *egeiro* means to be raised from the dead, awaken, collect one's faculties, and be raised from inactivity. *Jesus saith unto him,* **Rise** *(egeiro), take up thy bed, and walk. And immediately the man was made whole, and took up his bed, and walked* (John 5:8–9). Jesus raises a lame man from inactivity as his legs are dead. *Wherefore he saith,* **Awake** *(egeiro) thou that sleepest, and* **arise** *from the dead, and Christ shall give thee light* (Ephesians 5:14). The Apostle Paul is telling people to arise from the death of slothfulness and inactivity; many today need to "wake up" from their lethargic Christian lifestyle.

The Greek word *allasso* means to change, transform, and be made different. *Behold, I shew you a mystery; We shall not all sleep, but we shall all be changed, In a moment, in the twinkling of an eye, at the last trump: for the trumpet shall sound, and the dead shall be raised incorruptible, and we* **shall be changed** *(allasso). For this corruptible must put on incorruption, and this mortal must put on immortality* (1 Corinthians 15:51–53).

The Greek word *athanasia* means everlasting, undying, and immortality. *So when this corruptible shall have put on* **incorruption** *(athanasia), and this mortal shall have put on* **immortality** *(athanasia), then shall be brought to pass the saying that is written, Death is swallowed up in victory. O* **death** *(thantos), where is thy sting? O grave, where is thy victory? (1 Corinthians 15:54–55).*

# Eternal Life and the God Kind of Life

Now that we understand the Greek words for life and eternal life, let's take a deeper look at some scriptures to understand what we have missed in the English translation.

*And this is the will of him that sent me, that everyone which seeth the Son, and believeth on him,* **may have everlasting life: and I will raise him up at the last day** (John 6:40). In English, we have combined the words everlasting and life into one word. By doing this, we have made this scripture only about everlasting life after we die in the future. In Greek, they are separate words — *aionios*, everlasting *eternal, forever, perpetual, and future;* and *zoe,* the God kind of life, which is for now before we die. Many have put off eternal life for the future and are unaware of the life available now. I encourage people not to wait until they die to see if they have eternal life. Practice with *zoe*, the God kind of life now, and be assured of life eternal after death.

## The Most Famous Verse

*That whosoever* **believeth** *in him should not* **perish***, but have* **eternal life***.*

*For God so loved the world, that he gave his only begotten Son, that whosoever* <u>believeth</u> *in him should not* **perish,** *but* **have everlasting life** (John 3:15–16). As we look at each word in this scripture in Greek, more truth comes to light. As we **believe**—trust in, cling to and rely on Him, we will not **perish**—cast off restraint and stay on the course of life. The word *have* in this verse means we hold the ability for possession for life *(zoe)* and everlasting *(aionous)*.

## Jesus Continues with More Precise Greek Words—Zoe, Aionous

*Verily, verily, I say unto you, He that **heareth my word, and believeth** on him that sent me, **hath everlasting life**, and shall not come into condemnation; but **is passed from death unto life*** (John 5:24). If you are hearing His Word and believing Him, then you can possess the God kind of life now and life eternal. The word *passed* in Greek is *echo,* which means *now in possession and condition and relationship of zoe*. You can pass from death *(thanatos)* to life *(zoe)*.

This is an excellent time to remind you of this book's primary phrase and theme. "Let the Word become life in your life!" Let the Word become life *(zoe)* in your life *(chay, nephesh, psuche)*!

## The Dead Hear His Voice and Live!

*Verily, verily, I say unto you, The hour is coming, and **now is, when the dead shall hear the voice of the Son of God**: and **they that hear shall "live."*** (John 5:25). This is another verse that many put into the future and interpret as the resurrection from the dead being the last day. However, Jesus clearly says that the hour is "now is." How many in the church have been dead to the things of God? How many can hear His voice speaking to them today? When we hear a "now" voice of God speaking to us, now, we will live *(zoe)*. Many in the church believe they will have eternal life after they physically die but do not know they can have *zoe* life today. Your natural life *chay, nephesh, and psuche* can be made alive with *zoe* today. The sky will be bluer, the grass greener. You will have a new purpose, and you will be awakened and come to your senses.

The *zoe* God kind of life will produce the fruit of the spirit in your life. Love, joy, peace, long-suffering, gentleness, goodness, Faith, meekness, and temperance cannot be produced with the natural life of *chay, nephesh, and psuche*. I encourage my ministers to get up on Monday morning and ask the Father what He wants to do in their harvest field that week. The Father will faithfully give you a new specific word that the dead at your workplace will hear and live. Religious rhetoric will not interest anyone, but a Word from God will awaken them to know that God is real and speaking to their lives. You may say, I have to be about my business for the week, but if you decide to be about the Father's business, He will also be about your business and will give you supernatural wisdom for the day.

## The Path to Zoe, the God Kind of Life Before Death

Don't forget to apply the Three Aspects of Faith we learned in chapter 1 as we journey on the path to the God kind of life. The Apostle Paul shares practical wisdom with the Romans. *Know ye not, that **to whom ye yield yourselves servants to obey**, his servants ye are to whom ye obey; whether of **sin unto death**, or of **obedience unto righteousness**? But God be thanked, that ye were the servants of sin, but ye have obeyed from the heart that form of doctrine which was delivered you. Being then made free from sin, ye became the servants of righteousness* (Romans 6:16–18). You become and have the kind of life you obey and yield to. When you hear, believe, and obey the Word, you become and have *zoe*. When you, as a servant, are in right standing with the Father, you will experience and enjoy the God kind of life now in this life and also be assured of eternal life after death.

# The Power of Death

After Jesus raised Lazarus from the dead, many Greeks heard about the miracle and told His disciples they wanted to see Jesus. Jesus responded with a parable explaining how transformation in one's life will draw many to them as a witness of the power of God. He explained how death to self has the capability of transformation. *Verily, verily, I say unto you,* **Except a corn of wheat fall into the ground and <u>die</u>, it abideth alone: <u>but if it die,</u> it bringeth forth much fruit** (John 12:24). The Greek word for die is *apothnesko* which means to die off; to be dead to; be slain; put off in place, time, or relation; separation; departure; cease; die. Many do not have fruit because they have not yet died to their self-life, the *chay, nephesh, and psuche* natural kind of life. Though they are still trying to be a witness and do good things in their natural life, they cannot do God's things. When we die to ourselves, we will bring forth the fruit of the God kind of life and will begin winning souls. Are you tired of not bringing forth fruit, then consider the power of death to self.

Jesus continues in the next verse and clarifies that He is talking about dying to the natural self-life. ***He that loveth his life (psuche) shall lose it,*** *and* ***he that hateth his life (psuche) in this world shall keep it unto life (zoe) eternal (aionios)*** (John 12:25). Everyone is tired because they are busy saving their life with the cares of this world, the deceitfulness of riches, and the lust of other things. If you put your desires and appetites before God, you'll lose them because they won't satisfy you anymore, and you'll begin looking for other things for satisfaction. If you put your business first before God, you will lose it, and it will not be blessed. You need to hear from God to inject the God kind of life into it. Husbands, if you continue to put your wife before God, you'll lose the God kind of life in the marriage and her. A marriage built on only the natural energy of events and activities, not the Word of God and His purpose for your lives, will become dull, and you'll soon be looking for another. Parents, if you put your children before God, you will lose the God kind of life and them. You can give them everything they want, but they will never be satisfied. Why? Because you're training them to enjoy the natural life *(psuche)* before death to self, which they will lose for eternity! Train them up in the ways of the Lord, and they won't depart. I know dying to yourself sounds scary, but once you find this new life of *zoe*, the old life will soon become boring compared to the life that God has planned for you.

The best example I can give you is in Genesis with Adam and Eve. Eve came to Adam and said, "I found a way to make our life *(psuche)* better with the tree of the knowledge of good and evil." You know the story; they both lost it all. They could have chosen the Tree of Life.

Jesus concludes the answer to the disciple's question about how honor and fame come. *If any man serve me, let him follow me; and where I am, there shall also my servant be: if any man serve me,* **him will my Father honour** (John 12:26). The Father cannot and will not honor you when you're serving other gods, other things, and serving your natural life.

When Jesus was teaching His disciples about how he was to die, Peter rebuked Him. Jesus then rebuked Peter by saying he was not promoting God's will but only that which pleases man. Jesus explained with a parable. *For* **what shall it profit** *a man, if he shall **gain the whole world**, and **lose his own soul**? Or what shall a man give in exchange for his soul?* (Mark 8:36–37). Many make it their goal to have their "best life now." The best natural life now cannot compare to the God kind of life. The natural life will end; the God kind of life will never end.

The Apostle Paul knew the power of death to self and explained baptism on a deeper level. *Know ye not, that so many of us as were baptized into Jesus Christ were **baptized into his death**? Therefore, we **are buried** with him by baptism into death: that like as Christ **was raised** up from the dead by the glory of the Father, even so, **we also should walk in newness of life*** (Romans 6:3–4). Have you been baptized into death, or did you only get wet? When we understand the power of dying to self, we will be raised to the God kind of life and begin walking in this new way of living. I remember an old song we used to sing in church: "I found a New Way of living . . . love, joy, health, peace; He has made them mine . . . power and victory, abiding in the vine."

## The Apostle Paul Embraces the Power of Death

The Apostle Paul does not fear death to self-life but embraces death to self-daily. *I protest by your rejoicing which I have in Christ Jesus our Lord; **I die daily*** (1 Corinthians 15:31). Paul tells us he dies *apothnesko (be dead to; put off; be slain; put off in place, time, or relation; separation; departure; cease; and die —* to self and the natural life daily). The cares of this life, the deceitfulness of riches, and the lust of other things come to you daily, but you must put them off and be dead to them. Paul followed the principle of the seed, going into the ground and dying so he could bring forth fruit. Suppose the Apostle Paul, who wrote half of the New Testament, had to die daily to self; where does that leave us; maybe hourly. Paul got up every day and said, I'm separating myself from the natural desires and temptations of self-life so I can walk in the God kind of life.

I often think about the old western movies where the cowboy would shoot fifteen times with his six-shooter. He would fall, then rise again and shoot, fall down, then rise and shoot again before falling down for the last time. That is like trying to die to ourselves; we keep rising repeatedly. If we would realize that every day we don't die to ourselves is one less day of living the God kind of life, maybe we would just let it go and let the transformation that the power of death can work in our lives.

In writing to the church at Corinth, the Apostle Paul explains how the god of this world has blinded the eyes and minds of the believers and has prevented them from walking in the light and truth of the glorious gospel. He explained that we preach Christ and not ourselves. *But **we have this treasure in earthen vessels**, that **the excellency of the power may be of God, and not of us**. We are troubled on every side, yet not distressed; we are perplexed, but not in despair; Persecuted, but not forsaken; cast down, but not destroyed; Always bearing about in the body the **dying** of the Lord Jesus, that **the life** also of Jesus might **be made manifest in our body**. For we which live are always delivered unto death for Jesus' sake**, that the life also of Jesus might be made manifest in our mortal flesh**. So then **death worketh in us**, but **life in you*** (2 Corinthians 4:7–12). We see here that the power of death is working in us, and the power of life is also working in us. Each day presents an opportunity to die to self so that life *(zoe)* can manifest in our mortal flesh. We will face trouble, distress, perplexing situations, persecution, and despair, but we are not destroyed and will not quit because the excellency of the power of God is in us.

### Oh, Death, Where Is Thy Sting?

The scripture has taught about the different kinds of life and the different kinds of death. We have learned that we can have the God kind of life superseding the natural life after death to self in the here and now. What about the death of our mortal body that we will all face someday? The Apostle Paul gives us a beautiful, comforting passage to continue our journey until that day. *So, when this corruptible shall have put on incorruption, and this mortal shall have put on **immortality**, then shall be brought to pass the saying that is written, **Death is swallowed up in victory. O death, where is thy sting? O grave, where is thy victory?** Therefore, my beloved brethren,* ***be ye stedfast, unmoveable, always abounding in the work of the Lord, forasmuch as ye know that your labour is not in vain in the Lord*** (1 Corinthians 15:54–58). You don't need to fear the death of self. You don't need to fear the death of your mortal body. Just be steadfast, unmovable, always abounding in the *zoe* God kind of life now, and you will be assured of eternal life forever.

## We Will Overcome Death

The Apostle John wrote the gospel of John, three Epistles, and after they tarred and feathered him but could not kill him, he wrote his last epistle to the seven churches. We can be confident he knew something powerful about life and death.

***He that hath an ear****, let him hear what the Spirit saith unto the churches; He that **overcometh** shall not be hurt of **the second death*** (Revelation 2:11). You have an ear to hear what the Spirit has been saying about life and death, you are overcoming your adversities, and will not be hurt by the second and final death.

***And they overcame him*** *by the blood of the Lamb, and by the word of their testimony;* ***and they loved not their lives unto the death*** (Revelation 12:11). You are an overcomer because of the blood of the Lamb, the word of your testimony, and loving not your natural *chay, nephesh,* and *psuche* life and are prepared for death. After you have lived the *zoe* kind of life and reached your final moment, you will transition into Eternal Life with God.

*And God shall wipe away all tears from their eyes; and* ***there shall be no more death****, neither sorrow, nor crying, neither shall there be any more pain: for the former things are passed away* (Revelation 21:4). As the old hymn says, what a day of rejoicing that will be!

## How Can You Know If You Have Life After Death?

*These things have I written unto you that believe on the name of the Son of God;* ***that ye <u>may know that ye have eternal life</u>****, and that ye may believe on the name of the Son of God* (1 John 5:13). The literal Greek reads this way; These things I have written unto you that believe you may know that the life *(zoe the God kind of Life)* you have is eternal *(aionous)*.

If you want to be sure you have eternal life, start with *zoe*, the God kind of life now.

Let the Word become life in your life.

## Questions:

- What kind of life do you have before death?
- What kind of life do you have after death?
- What kind of life do you have after death to self?
- How often did the Apostle Paul say you must die to the self-life?
- What assurance do you have for life after death?
- How many Christians do you recognize who are missing out on the *zoe* God kind of life now and only waiting for eternal life after their physical death?
- Do you have Faith in the God kind of life now by dying to the self-life?
- Do you have Faith in eternal life after death?
- What was the most significant revelation you received while reading this chapter?

## Prayer Focus:

- Pray that you will see and recognize the different kinds of life (*chay, nephesh, psuche, zoe,* and *anastasis*).
- Pray that you will see and recognize the different kinds of death (*maveth, ratsach, teleute, thanatos,* and *epithanatios*).

- Pray that you will recognize the kind of life people are living today.

- Pray that you will recognize what kind of death people are experiencing today.

- Pray that you will experience the two kinds of life available in John 3:16.

- Pray that as you hear the Word, you will experience the *zoe* God kind of life today.

- Pray that you will experience the *zoe* God kind of life after you die to yourself.

- Pray that you will make "I die daily" a daily lifestyle.

- Pray that your fear of death will be eliminated as you understand the power of death.

- Pray that you will have the Faith to overcome by the blood of the Lamb, the word of your testimony, and love not your life unto the death.

- Pray that you will have the *zoe* God kind of life today and life eternal.

# CHAPTER 14

# Faith for Forgiveness

As we begin this chapter, please read this confession aloud: *"I can have everything the Bible says I can have, I can be everything the Bible says I can be, and I can do everything the Bible says I can do. Today I'm going to let the Word become life in my life."*

I remember when I was preparing to speak at a meeting of pastors in my city, and I asked the Lord what He wanted me to talk about. I was surprised when He said, "Forgiveness!" I thought forgiveness was silly and too simple to speak to pastors about. After all, what pastor would not understand forgiveness as it is the gospel 101? I wanted some super spiritual topic and great revelation that they possibly had not heard yet, but I have learned to trust and go with what the Lord says. I began a search for forgiveness in the Bible and found fifty-three verses; we could say one for each week of the year and still have an extra one, just in case. Forgiveness is a central theme of the gospel and is a must to understand completely. I compiled a few verses for the pastors' meeting and shared some scenarios on how we must apply and walk in forgiveness. At the end of the pastors' session, many were crying and praying for forgiveness for themselves, the people in their congregation, and their family members. The Lord knew what they needed to hear, so we must also hear about Faith for forgiveness.

## The Power of Forgiveness

A famous portion of scripture comes from the Sermon on the Mount when Jesus taught his disciples many things concerning the Kingdom of God. In Matthew chapter 5, Jesus talks about the poor in spirit, those that mourn, the meek, the hungry, the merciful, the pure in heart, the peacemakers, and those that are persecuted. He continues to tell them that they are the salt and light that God has called to be a witness of His Kingdom on the Earth. In chapter 6, He teaches about the will of God and how forgiveness is necessary for their ministry.

*Thy kingdom come.* ***Thy will be done in earth****, as it is in heaven. Give us this day our daily bread.* *And* ***forgive us our debts, as we forgive our debtors****. And lead us not into temptation, but* ***deliver us*** *from evil: For thine is the kingdom, and the power, and the glory, for ever. Amen.* ***For if ye forgive*** *men their trespasses, your heavenly Father will also* ***forgive you: But if ye forgive not*** *men their trespasses****, neither will your Father forgive your trespasses*** (Matthew 6:10–15). Jesus begins with communicating that it is the will of God to provide for you as His minister in the Kingdom daily. He then shares the power of forgiveness and the warning of not walking in forgiveness. I have heard many say, "God will never forgive me; I have done too many bad things." No, no, and again I say no. Please understand and settle it in your heart that it is the will of God to forgive you! God sent Jesus to pay the price for your forgiveness so God can and will forgive you. Jesus then says forgiveness involves a combination of God forgiving us *as* we forgive others. The only way we can forgive others is by understanding how and why God has forgiven us, and that is by Grace and not because we have or will do everything right. Every time we forgive someone, we remember God forgives us by His Grace. When Jesus said to lead us not into temptation but deliver us from evil, I wonder if He referred to the temptation not to forgive and how evil it is not to forgive. How many times have you been tempted not to forgive someone?

## Forgive Sin

In Matthew 6:12, Jesus uses words such as debts, debtors, and trespasses. The Greek word for debts is *opheilema*, which means something owed, a fault, or a moral failure. The Greek word for debtors is *opheiletes* which means delinquent, morally failing in duty, a transgressor against God, or a sinner. The Greek word for trespasses means to slip, lapse, deviation, sin, error, and willful offense. All these words come from the root word *hamartia,* which means to miss the mark, not to share in the prize, fault, offend, and to offend. We can see that Jesus is not just talking about a late payment or someone walking on your lawn; it is deeper in the heart and actions and produces moral and spiritual failure.

The Apostle Paul writing to the Romans corrects them about their pride and religious behavior and how many thought they were better than others because of their belief.

***For all have sinned and come short of the glory (honor) of God*** (Romans 3:23). Can you always hit the "bullseye?"

Sin is simply missing the mark, missing the center of God's will and purpose for your life. When we get past the word *sin*, meaning smoking, drinking, murder, and kicking the cat, we will realize that we miss the mark, and so does everyone else. The critical thing to see is that when we miss the mark, we fall short of the glory of God. The Greek word for glory is *doxa* and it means the dignity, honor, praise, and pleasing of God. God is not mad at you for missing the mark; but He can't honor and praise you. His will is to honor and praise you as this pleases Him. His will is for you to hit the mark, which may take some practice, but you will get better at your aim. Receive your forgiveness, pick up the Word of God as an arrow, and shoot again. God loves to see you practice until you become a pro.

After pastoring for forty years, I have seen a lot of people missing the mark, and yes, I've missed the mark, too. Sometimes I wonder if some people even know what and where the target is as I find them shooting at each other. What should I do? Forgive them and preach another Word of God archery lesson on what and where the target is, how to hit the mark of the prize of the high calling in Christ Jesus, and watch God honor them (See Philippians 3:14). Today we have the "everybody gets a trophy" mindset, but that is not biblical. The world is training people with this mindset that you don't have to do anything or be responsible and yet you still think you are entitled. If the world honors you, it will be for a moment, but if God honors you, it will be for a lifetime.

## Forgive

The Greek word for forgive is *aphiemi* and it means to lay aside, leave, let alone, let be, let it go, send, to go, send forth, forgive, forsake, omit, put away, send away, remit, suffer and yield up. All these definitions are robust, but the one I like the best is "just let it go!" If you hold on to pain, anger, or disappointment, it will progress into bitterness, becoming a root that is almost impossible to get out of your heart (see Hebrews 12:21). I have had to minister to people who have held on to unforgiveness for years because of something someone did to them in their childhood. I can't imagine how painful that is, but I would tell them, do you realize the person that did that to you is dead and in the grave? Why would you allow them to ruin your life today from the grave? Let it go, forgive them, be free, and enjoy the life God has for you now. If you don't forgive others, you might be the one who pays more dearly. I trust you see that no matter what someone does to you, just "let it go" and forgive. Settle in your heart right now; I will be a forgiver, forgiven, and honored by God. Many are unwilling to forgive someone out of fear that that person will hurt you again — and they may hurt you again — but the power of forgiveness will keep you free from that hurt and bitterness trying to take root in your heart.

## How Often Do I Forgive?

Jesus is teaching forgiveness, and Peter comes up to Him and asks the question we all want to ask. I love how Peter is always the first to jump in, so we can sit back and see how it turns out.

*Then came Peter to him, and said,* ***Lord, how oft shall my brother sin against me, and I forgive him? Till seven times?*** *Jesus saith unto him,* ***I say not unto thee, Until seven times: but, Until seventy times seven*** (Matthew 18:21). I am sure Peter thought by suggesting seven times that he would sound super spiritual and impress Jesus; we may also think seven times is a lot. Peter was speechless, as we were when we heard the response Jesus gave. Jesus says, I say not seven times but seven times seventy! If you do the math, that comes out to 490 times, which applies to just one person. How many other people do you have in your life that you will need to forgive? Jesus is not saying that 490 times is the required number of times to forgive someone but simply that forgiveness is the will of God and a biblical principle that must become a way of life. It looks like the Word forgiveness needs to "become life in our life" as a daily lifestyle!

Because Jesus requires us to forgive others 490 times, we know that God will also forgive us daily, no matter how many times we need forgiveness. When we fail God, fall short, and miss the mark, we get tired and ashamed of asking God for forgiveness again. Some have said, I have failed so many times; I don't want to get back up only to fall again. But, if you don't get back up, you have already failed. The best way to fail is to do nothing — then, you're guaranteed failure. God is pleased when you admit you failed; he will step in and forgive you, say let me help you, and I'll show you how to hit the target next time.

## Jesus Demonstrates Forgiveness

In Luke, chapter 23, we find how Jesus demonstrates forgiveness. The chief priests vehemently accused Him; they scourged Him with thirty-nine stripes on His back, plucked the hair out of His beard, placed a crown of thorns on His head, and nailed Him to a cross through His hands and feet. If anyone had the right not to forgive, it was Jesus. After all, He had done nothing wrong to deserve any of it. Jesus is hanging on a cross after all this horrendous punishment, and He opens His mouth and says, **Father, forgive them; for they know not what they do** (Luke 23:34). This is the most amazing, extreme, and ultimate demonstration of forgiveness that goes beyond our imagination. Jesus could have called ten thousand angels, but because of His love for them, you, and me, He used His will and the power of forgiveness to complete His mission to pay the price for our every sin. The next time someone says or does something to you, compare it to what Jesus went through, and it will seem ridiculous to hold a grudge and easy to quickly forgive.

When Jesus asked the Father to forgive them, He said it was because "they know not what they do." The words "know not" in Greek means, can't perceive or understand even with wide open eyes. They looked at Jesus hanging on the cross with wide open eyes but still could not perceive or understand what He was doing for them. It is hard for me to believe sometimes that people don't know what they're doing, but Jesus clarified that they could not perceive or understand even when they saw the stripes on His back and His sacrifice for their sins. The Apostle Paul explains to the church at Corinth, why the lost cannot see, *But if our gospel be hid, it is hid to them that are lost: In whom* **the god of this world hath blinded the minds** *of them which believe not, lest the light of the glorious gospel of Christ, who is the image of God, should shine unto them* (2 Corinthians 4:3–4). Paul says their minds in **Greek noema,** which means perception, purpose, intellect, and thought.

People do not know what they're doing because the god of this world has hidden the gospel, and they cannot comprehend the things of God without the light of the gospel. Paul continues with the answer. *For **we preach not ourselves**, but Christ Jesus the Lord; and ourselves your servants for Jesus' sake. For God, who commanded the light to shine out of darkness, hath shined in our hearts, to give the light of the knowledge of the glory of God in the face of Jesus Christ. But **we have this treasure in earthen vessels**, that the excellency of the power may be of God, and not of us* (2 Corinthians 4:5–7). We will never change anyone by arguing with them why they are wrong, and we are right. We need to forgive them, preach Christ, and give them the light of the knowledge of the glory of God. You have this treasure in you; if you forgive, serve, and preach, the light will shine in them.

## Forgiveness Takes Practice

It has been said that practice makes perfect, which applies to learning how to walk in a lifestyle of forgiveness. I confess that, initially, I was a little crude when I started this forgiveness principle. I would say, "Father forgive them because they're idiots." I graduated to "Father forgive them because they don't have a clue of what they are doing." Before you judge me, let me just tell you that I had to start somewhere — and so will you. The good news is that I finally made it to having a heart of compassion for those who had wronged me and understood they could not possibly change without love and an actual demonstration of forgiveness. I understood that God was not calling me a stupid idiot because I didn't know what I was doing but loved, forgave, and shined His Word in my heart. We must practice forgiving others like our Heavenly Father has forgiven us. Keep practicing, and forgiveness will become a natural lifestyle.

## Trying to Pray Without Forgiveness

The principle of forgiveness begins in our prayer time. Jesus taught that God's house should be called a house of prayer, giving us a powerful truth to understand when we're praying. *And **when ye stand praying, forgive, if ye have ought against any**: that your Father also which is in heaven may forgive you your trespasses. **But if ye do not forgive**, neither will your Father which is in heaven forgive your trespasses* (Mark 11:25–26). How can we accurately pray for someone if we have an attitude against them or are offended by them? I wonder what God thinks when we spend our time in prayer complaining to Him about someone and how we want Him to change them. How often do families come to church to worship God right after a fight with their spouse, yell at the children in the car's back seat, and then walk in acting Holy and ready to worship? Every prayer, praise, and worship service may need to begin with forgiveness, as this is the perfect time to practice forgiveness and the freedom it brings.

## What Forgiveness Is Not

In trying to understand what something is, we must first understand what it is not. We need to eliminate the false ideas and beliefs about what true forgiveness is.

Forgiveness is not:

- Approving or diminishing sin
- Enabling sin
- Denying wrongdoing
- Waiting for an apology
- Forgetting

- Ceasing to feel pain
- About getting another person to change

If you forgive someone, it does not mean you approve of their sin or diminish what they did. Today's world thinks everybody's OK. No, everybody's still not OK. They've still sinned, fallen short, and missed the mark, which is unacceptable. Forgiveness is not diminishing sin so they get a lower sentence just because you forgive them; they're still in the same condition. Until they ask for forgiveness, they're still in their sin.

If you forgive someone, it does not mean you are enabling their sin because you forgive them. They cannot do it again, and it will be OK. You're forgiving them for their sin, not saying it's accepted behavior from now on.

If you forgive someone, it does not deny the wrongdoing ever happened; they will still have the consequences because of their sin; forgiving them will simply free you from it affecting you.

Forgiving someone is not waiting for their apology to complete your forgiveness, as that may never come. Jesus forgave the Roman soldiers; they did not apologize but continued to crucify Him. The time will come when they ask God for forgiveness. The same thing may happen with your person. They may come back to you years later, apologize, and ask you for forgiveness, but until then, you let it go.

If you forgive someone, it does not mean that you'll ever forget it. I have heard people say you will know when you've forgiven by when you forget it. Our memory is impressive; it won't be long before the enemy reminds you of the wrongdoing. The next time you see that person, you will remember, but now you will immediately forgive again. Remember what Jesus told Peter about 490 times. The victory here is that even though you don't forget the trespass, and you do remember it, you still have a heart of forgiveness that will free you.

If you forgive someone, it does not mean you won't feel the pain they caused, but the power of forgiveness will cause that pain to turn into a pang of compassion for them and the condition they're in. I wonder if Jesus still feels pain each day when someone rejects Him and the price He paid for them.

Forgiving someone does not mean you'll get them to change, either. Forgiveness is not about getting another person to change; it is about obeying God's will to walk in forgiveness and be free from offenses, hurts, and pain they have caused in your life. Let the Word of forgiveness become life in your life today!

## Where Do We Start with Forgiveness?

As with any topic in the Bible, we must start with Faith in what God has said about it in His Word. Forgiveness is Bible 101, the foundational principle for our new life in Christ. In his first epistle, the Apostle John tells us that the Word of Life was manifested in Jesus, and we have heard and seen with our eyes how Jesus lived the God kind of life in the flesh. He continues with how we can have fellowship with the Father and walk in the light as the blood of Jesus cleanses us from all sin and darkness. He warns us not to be prideful, thinking that we will never sin and end up deceiving ourselves, for all have sinned and missed the mark. The instructions are evident when we sin. ***If we confess OUR sins, he is faithful and just to forgive us OUR sins and to cleanse US from all unrighteousness. If we say that we have not sinned, we make him a liar, and his Word is not in us*** (1 John 1:9–10). It is easy to see and confess someone else's sin, and most of us can do that every day, but it is another thing to see, admit, and confess our sins. We certainly do not commit murder, rape, or steal but remember that sin is missing the mark and falling short of the will of God. Did we witness today, pray for the sick today, yell at our spouse or kids today, and how about have a bad attitude and a pity party? Relax. We all have "bad days" and miss the mark, so confess what you've done, receive forgiveness, and restore your pure fellowship with your Heavenly Father. Instead of thinking that confessing our sin is a grueling task, consider one more time that we can fellowship with our Father and experience His love and forgiveness. The Greek word for forgiveness is *aphesis* and it means freedom, pardon, deliverance, liberty, remission, and bring back into purpose. Who would not want that list in their life every day?

## Different Scenarios of Forgiveness

The first scenario of forgiveness is when you confess your sin. You have Faith that God will forgive you, offer you freedom, liberty, and deliverance, and restore you to your purpose.

The second scenario of forgiveness is when you forgive someone else. You have Faith that God will release you from any hurt or disappointments they have caused you. When you forgive them, they can experience the freedom to restore their relationship with you. However, God has not forgiven them until they repent to God.

The third scenario of forgiveness is asking someone else to forgive you. You may need to practice the first two scenarios before you have the Faith to ask someone to forgive you. You may struggle with this level of forgiveness and find it challenging to have confidence in doing so. When you ask someone to forgive you, they can experience the freedom to restore their relationship with you and let go of the offense they have felt toward you. They may pass on the opportunity to forgive you, but you can now be free and accessible to them. Every time you humble yourself and ask someone to forgive you, the love of God and His compassion grows in you, and you become more like Christ.

The world is full of people holding on to bitterness, hurts of the past, and unforgiveness and will stay in that condition until forgiveness sets them free. God is looking for a person that understands His forgiveness and is willing to become a demonstration of forgiveness wherever you go. "Father, forgive them; they know not what they do."

## Questions:

- How did the definition of sin help you understand why the scripture says, "for all have sinned"?
- What stood out to you about the definition of forgive and forgiveness?
- How did Jesus's demonstration of forgiveness impact you?
- What are some of the things that forgiveness is not?
- How does a root of bitterness and unforgiveness cause us to fall short of the glory and honor of God?
- Which of the three scenarios of forgiveness changed your life?

- How did Jesus's response to Peter about forgiving 490 times impact you?
- Why does it take Faith to walk in forgiveness?
- What was the most significant revelation you received while reading this chapter?

## Prayer Focus:

- Pray that you will see and recognize the necessity to walk in forgiveness.
- Pray that you will see and recognize the power of forgiveness.
- Pray that you will understand how "let it go" is a simple way to forgive others.
- Pray that you will forgive 490 times daily until forgiveness becomes a lifestyle.
- Pray that you will remember how and when Jesus demonstrated forgiveness when faced with difficult hurts that are hard to forgive.
- Pray that you will not fall back into the list of things that forgiveness is not.
- Pray that you will make living by Faith a daily priority.
- Pray that you will recognize the three scenarios of forgiveness and which one is necessary for you to apply.
- Pray that you will not grow weary in confessing your sin by knowing forgiveness is always available.
- Pray that your Faith in forgiveness will grow stronger each day.

# CHAPTER 15

# Faith for the Future

As we begin this chapter, please read this confession aloud: *"I can have everything the Bible says I can have, I can be everything the Bible says I can be, and I can do everything the Bible says I can do. Today I'm going to let the Word become life in my life."*

Everyone, at one time or another, has wished they could know the future. People want to see the future to gather information about all sorts of topics. People are interested in details such as whether they'll be married or have children or what their job will be. They even want to know who will win the Super Bowl. People also have broader curiosities, such as what the economy will be like or whether there will be more world wars. They often wonder about when the end of the world will be or whether their children will be saved, how long they will live, when Jesus will return, and what they should invest in. Many will run to different sources, such as tea leaf readers, psychics, horoscopes, palm readers, prophets, and seers. I'm sure we've tuned into the weather forecasters to know how to prepare for the week. Even though many desire to see the future, some do not because they're afraid of what's coming and would instead take a que sera sera/

whatever will be will be mindset. What is a Christian to do regarding knowing the future? The Bible is full of prophecies that have already come to pass precisely, as predicted. Take the prophecy of the coming Messiah, for example. *And he said unto them, These are the words which I spake unto you, while I was yet with you, that all things must be fulfilled, which **were written in the law of Moses, and in the prophets, and in the psalms, concerning me*** (Luke 24:44). Jesus said that Moses, the prophets, and the Psalms prophesied of Him. Hundreds of prophecies in the scripture have already come to pass, so we can rest assured that the rest of the prophecies will also come to pass.

No matter your life stage, having Faith in your future is essential. When we don't believe God has a plan for us, we try to take control of our own lives, which usually leads to anxiety and many other sins. God has a perfect plan and purpose for your life, and you can know the future because Jesus said, *Howbeit when he, the Spirit of truth, is come, he will guide you into all truth: for he shall not speak of himself; but whatsoever he shall hear, that shall he speak: and **he will shew you things to come*** (John 16:13).

## Carve Out Rivers

Isaiah prophesies to the children of God and tells them God will bring them from the north, south, east, and west to make them His people created for His glory. He instructs them to **Remember** ye, **not the former things**, *neither consider the things of old. Behold,* **I will do a new thing**; *now it shall spring forth;* **shall ye not know it? I will even <u>make</u>** *a way* **in the wilderness, and <u>rivers in the desert</u>** (Isaiah 43:18–19).

God tells us to stop meditating on the past and see the new thing He will do in our life. Shall you not know it? God expects us to see the future and what He will do. The Greek word for make means to make a road, to carve out, and to make a flow.

In a Wednesday night service at BAM International, the Lord instructed me to take the shofar and drag it across the floor, carving a river before the altar. The Lord said He carved a river in our church, and all who would come into the river would be healed. Without saying anything, the people who went to the altar were slain in the Spirit and received healing and deliverance. I did not pray or lay hands on anyone as the Lord touched each one directly. Two weeks later, I scheduled The Feast of Tabernacles Camp meeting for our churches in the area. God honored His Word as people from thirteen different denominations attended the meetings each night for a week. Every night as people came to the altar, they were blessed, healed, and refreshed by a touch from God as they stepped into the river. Does God want to carve out a river in your city?

## The River of Past, Present, and Future

One morning, as I began my prayer time immediately, I was caught up in the spirit. I don't know how to explain this, but suddenly I was standing in front of a river, not in my chair anymore. I saw people standing in front of the river, and when they saw something floating down the river, they would reach in and try to grab it. By the time they got into the river, it was already downstream, and they felt terrible, disappointed, and ashamed that they didn't get in the river quickly enough to get it. I realized it was coming, but they weren't prepared for it when it got there because they only saw it when it was right in front of them. Then immediately, I was lifted up in the Spirit, looking down at the river and viewing the river from the sky. Immediately, the Lord said this is the river of past, present, and future. I had already seen what was right before me, but now I saw what was already downstream and what was coming down the stream. I could see the past, present, and future in this position. The Lord spoke to me and said He could see what is coming, what is, and what has been. He told me that He sees the past, present, and future all simultaneously and desires His people to be able to see it, also. Instantly I was back in my chair with thoughts going through my mind like a ticker tape of words passing in front of me. I will now do my best to relay what the Lord showed and explained.

## Seated in Heavenly Places

As I sat in my chair after this vision, meditating on what I had just experienced, the Lord reminded me of the scripture concerning being seated in heavenly places. *And you hath he quickened, who were dead in trespasses and sins; Wherein* **in time past ye walked according to the course of this world**, *according to the prince of the power of the air, the spirit that now worketh in the children of disobedience: Among whom also* **we all had our conversation in times past** *in the lusts of our flesh, fulfilling the desires of the flesh and of the mind; and were by nature the children of wrath, even as others. And* **hath raised us up** *together, and* **made us sit together in heavenly places** *in Christ Jesus:* **That in the ages to come he might shew** *the exceeding riches of his grace in his* **kindness** *toward us through Christ Jesus. For by Grace are ye saved through Faith; and that not of yourselves: it is the* *gift of God: Not of works, lest any man should boast. For we are his workmanship,* **created in Christ Jesus unto good works,** *which God hath before* **ordained that we should walk in them** (Ephesians 2:1–10). When people get together, their conversation usually begins with the past. They talk about the good old days, what they did when they were young, and the happy and sad times. Even if they talk about the latest news report, those events have already happened and are "downstream," and they can't do anything about them other than talk about them. The conversation proceeds to what they are doing the rest of the day based on their desires of the flesh and mind. When people talk about the future, their conversation is typically filled with fear of what might happen or a feeble wish of what they would like to happen. The Apostle Paul tells the church at Ephesus how to change this worthless conversation by understanding that we sit in heavenly places where we can see the past, present, and future. You don't need to stand in front of the river and only see what is present and past but be able to see what God is bringing to you by looking upstream into the future. God wants to show you the riches, the kindness, and the Grace coming down the river, but if we continue to look at the river of the present or past, we'll miss it.

Faith in the future is not blind hope when we sit in heavenly places. When we learn to sit in heavenly places in our prayer time, God will show us things to come. Faith in the future becomes trusting and preparing for what God has already shown you. We are created for good works and are ordained to walk in them, but we need to see what is coming, what He desires to do, and by Faith for the future, prepare to be a co-laborer with Him.

Over the years, I have traveled to Australia many times, preaching in several churches and overseeing the Bible school I established in the churches. I ministered in many cities throughout the country, but when preaching in churches on the Gold Coast, I couldn't help but try surfing. It was not long before the locals could see I was a newbie and were kind enough to sit down with me and give me some pointers. As we sat on the beach, they told me I had to understand that the waves come in sets of three. They said the first wave would die out quickly, the second wave is the one to catch, and a third wave is a washing machine that will give you a sinus cleansing while churning you upside down and then you'll find yourself on the bottom getting an exfoliant scrub from the sand. They said to study the waves sitting on the beach because they're easy to see from there and I would recognize them more quickly once I was out on the water. I thought, OK, I've got this, and out in the water I went. Sitting on my board, I was excited because I could see the three waves coming. As soon as I saw the second wave, I turned around and started paddling, but to my surprise, the wave went right underneath me, and I was still sitting there. I soon realized I needed to start paddling before the wave got to me to build momentum to catch it. When I finally figured out the timing, I caught the wave. It almost seemed supernatural, riding the wave and sailing with the wind. I share this example because it's the same principle as Faith for the future. As we sit in heavenly places, we will see the wave of God's plan coming; we turn around and start paddling and preparing for the good work He is about to do. If we wait to see it happening before us, we will miss it and watch it go by.

# What Is the Church Doing Today?

I hear many Christians testify about what God did in their life years ago, but rarely what God is doing in their life today. Their conversation continues about the past, whether about the good old days or disappointments when God did not seem to move in their life. Their discussion will then turn into complaints about the government, politics, the economy, and the sinners they work with. David sums up this type of conversation. ***By the rivers** of Babylon, there **we sat down, yea, we wept**, when **we remembered** Zion. **We hanged our harps upon the willows** in the midst thereof. For there they that carried us away captive required of us a song; and they that **wasted** us required of us mirth, saying, Sing us one of the songs of Zion. **How shall we sing the Lord's song in a strange land?*** (Psalm 137:1–4). They were sitting by the river but could only see the past downstream, how they missed it, and the hurt they felt, and they wept. They hung their praise instruments on the willows in the shallow and stagnant water because they had nothing to sing and praise the Lord for. If they only looked upstream and had Faith in the future, they would begin to praise God for what he was about to do.

# How Far Downstream Can You See?

One of the questions the Lord asked me when I was in the vision above the river was, "How far can you see downstream?" I tried to see what happened yesterday, last week, last month, last year and remembered a few things. He said, "No, look farther back to Genesis." I said I needed a little help with that, and He began to show me cycles of events that happened during the time of Adam and Eve, Noah, Moses,

Joshua, David, and Jesus. Each cycle contained a progressive list of events that occurred similarly. The list He gave me for each cycle was fall, darkness, void, judgment, redemption, creation, and reset. In Genesis, we can see it started with the fall of Satan, darkness was upon the Earth, and it became void of God's purpose. God judged it and brought redemption; He then created life and reset it with Adam and Eve to govern the Earth. The cycle started over again with the fall of man and progressively went through the list.

## The List of Cycles Beginning at Genesis and The Reset with a Type of Messiah

- Fall, darkness, void, judgment, redemption, creation, reset—**Adam and Eve**
- Fall, darkness, void, judgment, redemption, creation, reset—**Noah**
- Fall, darkness, void, judgment, redemption, creation, reset—**Moses**
- Fall, darkness, void, judgment, redemption, creation, reset—**Joshua**
- Fall, darkness, void, judgment, redemption, creation, reset—**David**
- Fall, darkness, void, judgment, redemption, creation, reset—**Jesus**

At the end of each cycle, God appointed a type of Messiah to reset His purpose for man on Earth. Many famous people played a part during each cycle, such as Abraham, Isaac, Jacob, Nehemiah, Isaiah, Jeremiah, Ezekiel, Daniel, Jonah, and Joel. Since the reset with Jesus, many such as Peter, Paul,

Matthew, Mark, Luke, John, and Timothy, have played a part in the cycle.

More recent people who have played a role in this cycle would be John Calvin, Martin Luther, Charles and John Wesley, William Branham, and others. Each person's gift and call would focus on a specific part in the cycle, such as teachers that would bring truth and light into the darkness, Prophets would bring judgment, pastors would bring redemption, apostles would create a new move, and evangelists would spread the good news of the Messiah.

King Solomon, the man God gave the gift of great wisdom, wrote the Proverbs, the book of wisdom. In his old age, Solomon looked back at the mistakes he had made in his lifetime and drew practical insight and an eternal perspective from them. Solomon experienced great success, failures, ups and downs in life, times of rejoicing, and disappointments. He began to see the cycles I've been discussing and wrote the book of Ecclesiastes. Some of the famous statements Solomon made were "All is vanity," "The Lord gives, and the Lord takes away," "There is a time for everything and a season for every activity under Heaven," "a time to be born and a time to die," "a time to weep and a time to laugh," "a time of war and a time for peace" to name a few. I believe he summed it up the best when he said, ***Generations come, and generations go, but the earth remains forever.*** *The sun rises, and the sun sets; it hurries back to where it arose. Blowing southward, then turning northward, round and round the wind swirls, ever returning on its course.* ***All the rivers flow into the sea****, yet* ***the sea is never full****; to the place from which the streams come****, there again they flow****. All things are wearisome, more than one can describe; the eye* *is not satisfied with seeing, nor the ear content with hearing.* **What has been will be again,** *and* **what has been done will be done again;** *there is nothing new under the sun. Is there a case where one can say,* **"Look, this is new"?** **It has already existed in the ages before us** (Ecclesiastes 1:4–10). Are you starting to see a pattern? Can you see the cycles constantly repeat themselves, and are you aware we are in the midst of a cycle right now?

## The Stream in Front of Us

As we stand at the stream before us, what part of the cycle is happening right now? If we look downstream, what part of the cycle has just passed by us recently? *For, behold, the* **darkness shall cover the earth,** *and* **gross darkness the people***: but the LORD shall arise upon thee, and his glory shall be seen upon thee* (Isaiah 60:2). Are we living in a time where many are in darkness and ignorant of the will and purpose of God? Many ungodly laws have been passed today, and people's lifestyles could be best described as "gross darkness," Jesus makes a statement about the condition of people just before the time that He is the Messiah that would start the reset. *For this* **people's heart is waxed gross,** *and* **their ears are dull of hearing,** *and* **their eyes they have closed;** *lest at any time they should see with their eyes, and hear with their ears, and should understand with their heart, and should be converted, and I should heal them* (Matthew 13:15). If we're paying attention, we should not be surprised and be able to see that the fall, darkness, and the void of His purpose have been passing by and going downstream right now.

### How Far Upstream Can You See?

Many believe the return of the Lord is soon, and we will experience the reset as Jesus sets up His Kingdom on the Earth, and we will rule and reign with Him for a thousand years. Until then, we must finish the rest of the cycle that is coming in the very near future. The next part of the cycle is judgment. *For the time is come that **judgment must begin at the house of God**: and if it first begin at us, what shall the end be of them that obey not the gospel of God?* (1 Peter 4:17). There have already been instances of prominent church leaders being judged for sins of adultery, misappropriation of funds, and abuse of authority. Many denominations have experienced judgment, and people are leaving because of the perverted doctrines they have adopted. When the church's judgment is complete, the world systems follow: government, sports, and entertainment are already experiencing judgment. As we continue to look upstream, we will see that redemption is next. *And **when these things begin to come to pass**, then look up, and lift up your heads; **for your redemption draweth nigh*** (Luke 21:28). If you see these things coming to pass, rejoice; our redemption is near.

## Faith for the Future Redemption, Creation, and Reset

Like the example I gave you of catching the waves in Australia, we see redemption coming, so we need to start paddling and preparing for it now. *Forasmuch as ye know that ye were **not redeemed with corruptible things**, as silver and gold, from your vain conversation received by tradition from your fathers; **But with the precious blood of Christ**, as* *of a lamb without blemish and without spot* (1 Peter 1:18). We cannot catch the wave of redemption with our own efforts, vain conversations, or the tradition of men, but only with the blood of Christ. The next wave to catch is creation. *Therefore, if any man be in Christ,* **he is a new creature***: old things are passed away; behold, all things are become new* (2 Corinthians 5:17). Start paddling to completely immerse yourself into Christ and let Him carry you to the final reset wave. *And* **I saw a new heaven and a new earth***: for the first heaven and the first earth were passed away; and there was no more sea. And* **I, John, saw the holy city, new Jerusalem***, coming down from God out of heaven, prepared as a bride adorned for her husband* (Revelation 21:1). What a glorious day that will be!

## Faith for the Future Eliminates Fear

As we journey through the last events of this cycle, we can have Faith in the future that will eliminate fear. Jesus said *These things I have spoken unto you, that in me ye might have peace. In the world* **ye shall have tribulation: but be of good cheer***; I have overcome the world* (John 16:33). During the phase of judgment and tribulation, if we are in Him, we will have peace that passes all understanding. We cheerfully know He has and will overcome the world and usher us into His Kingdom. *Thou art come to the kingdom for such a time as this?* (Esther 4:14). The church is living in its finest hour as it takes its part in walking out the events of this cycle. *And* **this gospel of the kingdom shall be preached in all the world for a witness** *unto all nations; and* **then shall the end come** (Matthew 24:14).

## Faith for The Future Activates Believers

Will you be an Ezekiel who prophesies judgment to the worldly mountains? (Ezekiel 36).

Will you be an Ezekiel who prophesies to the dry bones to live? (Ezekiel 37).

Will you be like the sons of Issachar who understood the times and became a part of the end-time army of God? (1 Chronicles 12).

Will you heed Isaiah's prophecy and take water to the poor and needy, open rivers in the desert, and plant in the wilderness? (Isaiah 41).

Will you follow Jesus and become a fisher of men? (Matthew 4:19).

Will you preach the gospel of the Kingdom to your world as a witness before the end comes? (Matthew 24:14).

I encourage you not to sit by the river and watch the workings of God pass you by. Each day, sit in heavenly places in prayer and see what God wants to do in and through you in your harvest field today. As you know what God wants to do, you can have Faith in the Future and never have another dull day complaining about what is or has been. Your Christian life will become exciting as you "let the Word become life in your life."

### A Few Last Scriptures to Build Your Faith for the Future

- *God is our refuge and strength, **a very present help in trouble**. Therefore **will not we fear**, though the earth be* removed, and though the mountains are carried into the midst of the sea; Though the waters thereof roar and be troubled, though the mountains shake with the swelling thereof. Selah. **There is a river, the streams whereof shall make glad the city of God,** the holy place of the tabernacles of the most High. **God is in the midst of her;** she shall not be moved: **God shall help her,** and that right early (Psalm 46:1–5).

- **And he shewed me a pure river of water of life,** clear as crystal, proceeding out of the throne of God and of the Lamb. **In the midst of the street of it, and on either side of the river, was there the tree of life,** which bare twelve manner of fruits, and **yielded her fruit every month: and the leaves of the tree were for the healing of the nations** (Revelation 22:1–2).

- And the Spirit and the bride say, **Come.** And let him that heareth say, **Come.** And let him that is athirst come. **And whosoever will, let him take the water of life freely** (Revelation 22:17).

- **Blessed is the man that trusteth in the LORD,** and whose hope the LORD is. For he shall be as a tree planted by the waters, and that spreadeth out her **roots by the river,** and shall **not see when heat cometh,** but her leaf shall be green; and shall **not be careful (worried)** in the year of drought, **neither shall cease from yielding fruit** (Jeremiah 17:7–8).

## Questions:

- How did my vision from the Lord help you see the past, present, and future?
- Has the time you sat in the past or even the present stolen your time from seeing the future?
- Give an example of how you have recognized that you have been sitting in the past.
- Why must we learn to sit in heavenly places consistently?
- What are the seven phases in a complete cycle of history?
- Is being able to see the future more straightforward than you thought?
- What does Faith for the Future mean to you now after this chapter?
- Who were the six types of Messiahs that God used at the beginning of the resets in history?
- How close are we to the next and most incredible reset?

## Prayer Focus:

- Pray that you will settle in your heart that you can have Faith in the future.
- Pray that you will let go of the past and set your Faith on the new thing God will show you.
- Pray that you will sit in heavenly places daily and see from God's perspective.

- Pray that you will understand that Faith in the future is not just blind hope.
- Pray that you will see clearly the list of events in each cycle.
- Pray that you will see clearly which event in the cycle you are now in.
- Pray that you will see the next event in the cycle God is about to manifest.
- Pray that the understanding of the time we live, the fear of the future, is eliminated as your Faith in the future becomes real.
- Pray that your Faith for the future will position you to be a part of what God is and is about to do.
- Pray that God will consider you one He will use to usher in the next reset.
- Pray that Faith for the future becomes a lifestyle.

# What's Next?

# BAM UNIVERSITY

### Classes from Born Again to Full-Time Ministry and Ordination

This is not the end of a message but rather the beginning of an ongoing relationship with Bill Anderson Ministries. If this book resonates with you on a spiritual level, BAM University may be the next step in your journey toward deepening your spiritual understanding and advancing your career in ministry.

## BishopBillAnderson.org/apply

# URGENT PLEA!

## Thank You for Reading My Book!

It would be greatly appreciated if you could take a moment to provide your feedback on my book by leaving a review on Amazon. Your insightful comments will serve as a valuable resource for improving future editions and ensuring that the content meets the needs and expectations of readers like you. Thank you in advance for your time and assistance in this matter.

## BishopBillAnderson.org/review

**Thanks so much,**

**Bishop Bill**

Made in the USA
Monee, IL
24 March 2024

f6f90a4b-4f7c-4b41-ae84-0eaecf728768R01